Randy Maxwell

Author of *If My People Pray*

Bring Back the GLORY

What happens when God's people pray—for revival

Pacific Press® Publishing Association
Nampa, Idaho
Oshawa, Ontario, Canada

Edited by Jerry D. Thomas
Art Direction and Design by Michelle C. Petz
Cover photo by Ed Guthero

ISBN 0-8163-1788-7

00 01 02 03 04 • 5 4 3 2 1

Dedication

To my three grandmothers—

Pearl "Mama" Jacobs, 1902 - 1998
Reva Bernice Owens, 1916 - 1996
Gertrude "Little Mother" Williams, 1907 -

—who reflected God's glory in their own lives
and left an enduring legacy of faith to their families.
Your children call you "blessed."

Other books by Randy Maxwell

If My People Pray

On Eagles' Wings

Loving is Fundamental

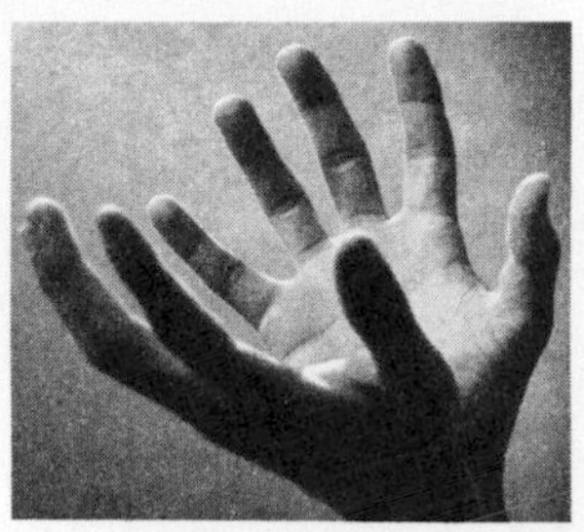

Contents

Restore us, O God Almighty; make your face shine upon us, that we may be saved. Revive us, and we will call on your name.
(Psalm 80:7, 18b, NIV)

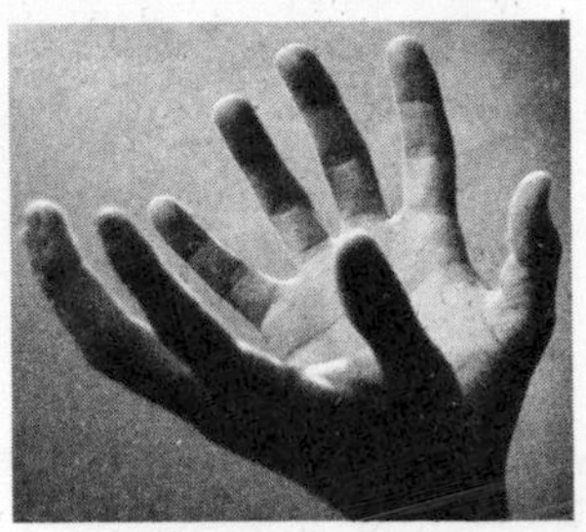

Acknowledgments

Writing a book is like birthing a child. Both activities require lots of love and support from family and friends. I'd like to thank a few members of my "support team."

To my spiritual mom (#2), Sister Patricia Langley and the Prayer Warriors of New York, your example keeps me going. I'm proud to be part of your family.

To my spiritual mom (#1), Ruthie Jacobsen, Thank you for calling me to the prayer ministry and believing in me. Only heaven knows the impact of your ministry around the world.

To Sister Lurline Brown, Thank you for sharing the 42-day fasting and prayer experience with me and with the thousands who will read about it in this book.

To my friend and reconciliation partner, Gary Botimer. Thanks for your support, vulnerability, example, and friendship. You are definitely a man of IMPACT!

To the Carnies (Jeff, Carole, Debra Griffin, and Richard Riley), you guys are awesome! I'll never be able to thank you enough for your encouragement, friendship, and help in making my other dream (the album) come true.

To my new "big sis" Margaret Finley who prays for me every Friday when I'm flying somewhere to lead another prayer conference. I appreciate your friendship and prayers so much.

To my friends and colleagues at Pacific Press who waited three years for this "baby" to be born. Thanks for hanging in there with me and yes, I forgive you for the merciless, daily harassment!

To my pastor, Stan Hudson, who listened to my ideas during the writing process, gave me input and prayed for me every Thursday when we got together for our weekly prayer and sharing time.

To my mom and dad, Shirley and Wilker Maxwell, who are my biggest fans and who prayed daily for God to help me birth this book. Here's your newest grandchild! Thanks for showing me the glory. I'm still your biggest fan.

To my daughters Candice, Crystal, and Danielle, who "lost" their father for several months to either the computer or United Airlines. Thanks for waiting, girls. Daddy's out of "the cave!" (For a while.)

To my bride Suzette, who prayed with me, read and critiqued the manuscript, and held my hand on those days I wanted to chuck the whole thing in the garbage and quit. I couldn't do this ministry without you, Sweetheart. Thanks for holding me and our family together. I love you.

And to my Friend and Savior Jesus Christ, who never ceases to amaze me with His grace, and who causes me to soar on eagles' wings. You have blessed me beyond all I could hope or imagine. Now show me your glory, Lord!

RKM

At this grim hour, the world sleeps in the darkness,
and the Church sleeps in the light.
–Leonard Ravenhill

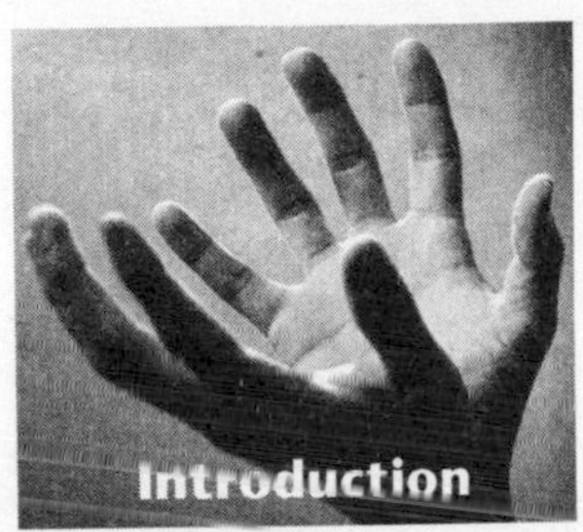

9:30 Living in a Midnight World

I woke with a start. My heart still raced as I fumbled in the darkness first for my glasses, then for a pad and pen. Snapping on the lamp, I quickly scribbled down the dream that had shaken me awake.

I seemed to have been in a large room where many theologians, evangelists, and ministers were gathered for some type of meeting. As I looked about the room, there were some impressive personalities there—some whose names are household words in our denomination. What I was doing among this gathering of preachers I don't know. But next thing I knew, I was asking a question. "What time is it?" I asked.

The men knew that I wasn't asking about the literal time, and one by one they began to hit me with every end-time cliché in the book. "It's nearly midnight," someone said. "We're living in the very toes of the image in Daniel 2," another shouted.

"No," I said with some degree of irritation. "That's not what I mean. I know these are the end times. What I want to know is where we are in the stream of time." Well, this attempt at clarification failed and I continued to get answers descriptive of the lateness of the hour. Finally, in frustration I said, "If Christ's second coming is represented by 'midnight,' then as far as our readiness to meet Him, where are God's people on that same clock?"

At that, one of the most prominent evangelists in that company looked right at me and said soberly, "Nine-thirty." The room fell silent, the impact of those words falling like a lead ball on the hearts and consciences of everyone present. *Though prophetically it is nearly "midnight" in the great controversy between Christ and Satan, God's people are living as though it were only 9:30!*

I suppose I could take comfort from the fact that this was just a dream and leave it at that. I could—if it weren't so true. Especially for me.

This book may be hard to read. It was certainly hard to write. Not because what I have to say is so deep and complex. It's just the opposite. What I have to say is simple and basic. And yet I shrink from the conclusions this book leads to. I have looked forward to getting these thoughts into print with equal amounts of excitement and fear. Excitement because I believe ours is the generation to receive the revival of true godliness that Ellen White described as the greatest of all our needs. Fear because the gulf between where I am and where God wants me to be spiritually is so great. *Because I'm living like it's only 9:30 when it's nearly midnight!*

Revival won't allow me to romanticize the altar. It calls me to die on it.

The subject of revival, so long a theme of my writing and preaching, an ideal and goal I've loved to talk and meditate on, makes me squirm the more I look into it. And yet I cannot turn away. Revival won't allow me to romanticize the altar. It calls me to die on it. Revival won't let me settle for "cheap grace"—that grace that Bonhoeffer says, "we bestow on ourselves" preaching forgiveness without requiring repentance. It demands my pursuit of "costly grace"—grace that includes a cross and the call to discipleship. Revival mocks my patchwork prayer life, questions my halfhearted commitment to Christ, rejects my compromises with sin, and wonders at my lack of compassion for the countless masses of men and women, boys and girls, who perish daily without knowing Jesus as their personal Savior.

I'll say it again. This book may be hard to read . . . and even harder to live with.

Revival—true biblical revival—is not what I thought it was. Play a little word association game with me for a moment. I recently watched a circus ringmaster lead an audience-participation game. He said "Big top." The crowd shouted back, "Circus!"

When I say "revival," what words and mental images come to your mind? Would you shout back "power!" or "miracles!" or "great preaching!" or "filled churches"? I would. But upon closer examination of the Book and the great revivals of the past, I realize that my musings are out of sync. These things are more often the *result* and not the *content* of revival.

"This is why," says James Burns, "a revival has ever been unpopular with large numbers within the church. Because it says nothing to them of power such as they have learned to love, or of ease, or of success; it accuses them of sin, it tells them that they are dead, it calls them to awake, to renounce the world, and to follow Christ."[2]

So why this book on this subject at this time? Why revival? Let me try to answer this with a similar question: Why a defibrillator in the E.R.? *To wake the dead!* To fire a heart that has gone cold. The church—no, I can't cop out with safe generalities—*I* am spiritually dead. *I* am indifferent to the lost souls all around me who don't know what I know. *I* am the one who is too busy to read my Bible, too tired to pray, too in love with ease and this world's comforts to put myself out for the kingdom. *I* am the "code blue" in heaven's emergency room, and I need the Holy Spirit to bring over His celestial "crash cart," yell "clear" and hit me with the faith-reviving paddles of life *now* to bring me back from the brink of spiritual death.

How about you?

I know that many of you who read this book are hungry for more of God in your lives. I know because I've talked with you and heard the "hunger pangs" in your conversation. There is a growing restlessness with "9:30 living in a midnight world."

Great. Let's not delay any longer.

In this book, I want to paint a picture of what can happen when God's people pray for revival. No two people look at the same painting and see the same things. But the basic content of the painting doesn't change. My purpose is to reveal the characteristics of the people Ellen White speaks of on page 69 of *Christ's Object Lessons*:

> *Christ is waiting with longing desire for the manifestation of Himself in His church.* When the character of Christ shall be perfectly reproduced in His people, then He will come to claim them as His own. (Emphasis added.)

This statement, so long burdened with perfectionist overtones, is really nothing more than an expression of longing on the part of Christ to see His heart beating in the chests of His children. He waits, as does nature itself[3], for His glory to be fully and finally revealed in you and me. "He waits," Chuck Swindoll says, "to be wanted. Too bad that with many of us, He waits so very long in vain."

I don't want to keep Him waiting any longer, do you? Time is running out. As I write this, another quake registering above seven points on the Richter Scale has rocked Taiwan. This is the fourth killer quake to rip across the surface of the earth in as many weeks. Hurricanes lash the islands of the Atlantic and flood previously drought-stricken states along the eastern seaboard. In what is being called the worst natural disaster to hit Venezuela this century, the death toll from the mudslides and flooding has surpassed 10,000 and is expected to rise. Random bombings are terrorizing Russia, and in America, hospitals and churches now join with schools as places that are no longer safe havens from wanton violence and mayhem. I believe these events are God's wake-up calls, and the time to respond to them is getting shorter all the time. It's not 9:30, people. It's nearly midnight.

Now is the time to pray Asaph's prayer, *Revive us, and we will call on your name.* Lord, bring the crash cart! Bring revival. Bring back the glory!

Randy Maxwell
Nampa, Idaho

---

1. C. William Fischer, *It's Revival We Need!* (Kansas City: Nazarene Publishing House, 1968), 12.
2. Romans 8:19.

"All things are yours"
(1 Corinthians 3:21).

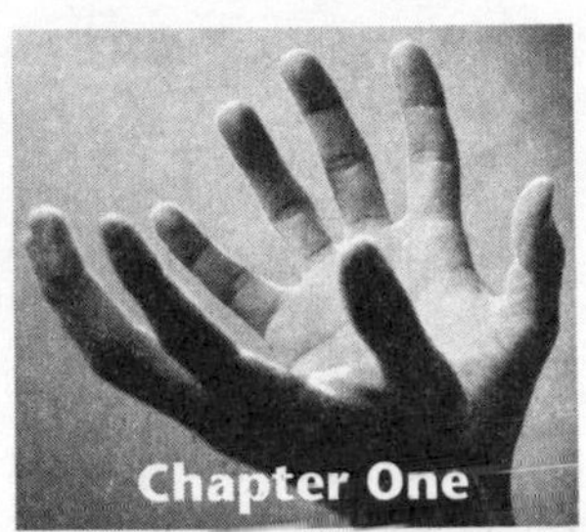

The Undiscovered Country

I admit it. I'm a *Star Trek* fan. A closet "Trekkie." I'm sure it has to do with the fact that as a boy, I dreamed of becoming an astronaut. The U.S. space program was about to put a man on the moon and I was caught up in the heady exuberance of discovery that has pushed people of all ages to leave familiar shores for new frontiers.

That sense of wonder was captured in the opening monologue of each *Star Trek* episode: "Our five-year mission—to explore strange new worlds; to seek out new life and new civilizations, to boldly go where no man has gone before!"

The real space men—the Apollo astronauts—were living out this fictional creed. They were to walk where no one had ever walked before. Theirs was to be an experience unshared by all but a few members of the human race. They were to see what no human eyes had seen; to hear what no other human ears had heard; to feel what had only been imagined in the minds of scientists, novelists, and pilots. These "Magellans of the late twentieth century" were to set foot, not on the distant shores of a new continent, but on the strange soil of another world!

First came Armstrong. His ghostly form lumbered down the stairs of his spider-like spacecraft, ironically named "Eagle," before his dramatic "leap for mankind" to the dusty lunar surface. I, like so many millions of others, was glued to the TV watching history unfold. What was it like to be 200,000 miles from home, watching not sun or moon, but *earth*—your earth—rise? Hear the words of General Charles Duke, pilot of Apollo 16, and one of only twelve men to walk on the moon.

> *None of us in the astronaut program volunteered for fame or fortune. If everybody was like me they volunteered for the thrill of adventure and sense of exploration. To see what it was like out there with your own eyes and your own feelings. It was just tremendously exciting to stand on the moon. I can't even put it into words the excitement I experienced as I stood there looking across this dramatic landscape which was absolutely lifeless. We just felt like we were supposed to be there. We did not feel like we were intruders in this foreign land.*[1]

The men of Apollo were visitors to an undiscovered country.

The western frontier

A hundred and twenty years before Armstrong's leap scratched America's itch to conquer the moon, the thrill of discovery, and the promise of wealth, was beckoning men west. Again, the bold and the brave risked all to follow the Oregon Trail to the sea. In the early 1840s, the West was the new frontier and the desire to get there drove a nation.

"Where did you go? West. Why? Just because. Magic. A thing of the spirit."[2] Adding to the lore of the times, Henry David Thoreau spoke of the beckoning Shangri-La in glowing terms. "The heavens of America appear [illegible]ly higher, the sky is bluer, the air is fresher, the cold is intenser, the moon looks larger, the stars are brighter, the thunder is louder, the lightning is vivider, the wind is stronger, the rain is heavier, the mountains are higher, the rivers longer, the forests bigger, the plain broader . . ."

"Will not man," Thoreau then asked, "grow to greater perfection intellectually as well as physically under these influences?"[3]

"Magic." "A thing of the spirit." Man achieving "greater perfection." These were the engines that drove the northwestern explorers to pursue their undiscovered country.

The Promised Land

Another time. Another place. Some three thousand years prior to the expeditions of Lewis and Clark, another scouting party was just coming back from a reconnaissance mission into the "undiscovered country" of Canaan. Twelve men from the tribes of Israel were chosen to explore this land of "milk and honey" God had promised to the descendants of Abraham nearly 700 years earlier.

The spies couldn't believe their eyes. For men who had only known the sting of the lash and the blood-stained mud of the Egyptian brick pits, the first glimpse of the Promised Land must have been breathtaking. The Bible records their early findings.

"When they reached the Valley of Eshcol, they cut off a branch bearing a single cluster of grapes. Two of them carried it on a pole between them, along with some pomegranates and figs" (Numbers 13:23, NIV).

Imagine grapes the size of cantaloupes! So heavy were these grapes that instead of carrying a cluster in one hand, it took two men to haul them away strapped to a plank. The land was rich and fertile, and abundant. And it was theirs for the taking. God had already promised it to them. But strange as it seems, some people had a hard time believing the promise.

"They came back to Moses and Aaron and the whole Israelite community at Kadesh in the Desert of Paran. There they reported to them and to the whole assembly and showed them the fruit of the land.

They gave Moses this account: 'We went into the land to which you sent us, and it does flow with milk and honey! Here is its fruit'" (Numbers 13:26, 27, NIV).

So far so good. If only they would have stopped there and possessed the promise! Yet something is amiss. The body language is wrong. Instead of bold confidence, there's a sag in the shoulders and you can hear the "but" that is sure to follow.

" '*But . . .*' " (Here it comes), " 'the people who live there are powerful, and the cities are fortified and very large' " (v. 28).

What's that noise? Sounds like knee caps banging together. Ah, but look. Not everyone's knees were knocking. Caleb, one of the twelve spies, tried to get the eyes of the crowd back where they belonged—on the God of the Exodus, the God who had brought them out of Egypt, through the Red Sea, and out of bondage with a "strong hand."

"Then Caleb silenced the people before Moses and said, 'We should go up and take possession of the land, for we can certainly do it'" (v. 30).

Within Caleb's chest beat a pioneer's heart. He, like Magellan, Lewis and Clark and Armstrong who would follow in future generations, wanted to possess the "undiscovered country." He was driven by a vision of a better life and by a belief in a God who so completely believed in him. Unfortunately, not everyone had "the right stuff."

"But the men who had gone up with him said, 'We can't attack those people; they are stronger than we are.' And they spread among the Israelites a bad report about the land they had explored. They said, 'The land we explored devours those living in it. All the people we saw there are of great size. We saw the Nephilim there (the descendants of Anak come from the Nephilim). We seemed like grasshoppers in our own eyes, and we looked the same to them.' That night all the people of the community raised their voices and wept aloud" (v. 31-14:1).

The record of what happened next is a sad chronicle of what happens [illegible] faith dies. When the thirsty traveler dies within sight of a well.

The Undiscovered Country

When the marathon runner collapses a few yards from the finish line. When the gambler sells the winning lottery ticket to a friend hours before the winning numbers are announced. *So close . . .*

The liberated sons and daughters of God, so recently rescued from the taskmaster's whip, cried out for the "security" of Egyptian slavery rather than put their trust in the promises of the God who swallowed Pharaoh's army in the Red Sea. Things may not have been great in Egypt, but at least they knew what to expect. Canaan was virgin territory—something altogether new. Their faith faltered and they lost it all.

"The Lord said to Moses, 'How long will these people treat me with contempt? How long will they refuse to believe in me, in spite of all the miraculous signs I have performed among them?. . . As surely as I live and as surely as the glory of the Lord fills the whole earth, not one of the men who saw my glory and the miraculous signs I performed in Egypt and in the desert but who disobeyed me and tested me ten times—not one of them will ever see the land I promised on oath to their forefathers' " (Numbers 14:11, 21-23).

The newly-freed slaves were turned away from the borders of the Promised Land and sentenced to wander in the desert for forty years—a year for each day the spies had explored the "undiscovered country" *without possessing it!*

Please note that they explored, sampled, walked through, investigated, observed, and gathered data on the Promised Land, but failed to possess it. They did not plant their flag on its soil. They did not go up and settle in.

For those twenty years old or more, their eyes would never see the land flowing with milk and honey. Their feet would never trod on its fertile soil. Their bodies would never find rest in the shade of Canaan's lush vineyards. Instead, their sun-scorched eyes and sand-blistered feet would know only the heat, monotony, and barrenness of the Judean wilderness. Until at last, their carcasses would fall in the desert; a mute testimony to the tragic consequences of unbelief and lack of vision.

The realm of the Spirit

In the sixth *Star Trek* film, the "undiscovered country" refers not to a place, but to a time. Specifically, the future. A future where old enemies lay down their weapons along with their hatred. A future filled with the hope and promise of peace—a dream as yet, unrealized, but within the grasp of those brave enough to pursue it.

For you and for me, our "undiscovered country" also refers to a time and an experience. The experience is personal and corporate spiritual revival. A return to our first love with Jesus, a rekindled hunger and thirst for the things of God, for communion with Him through His Word, worship, and prayer. A reawakened sense of urgency regarding our Lord's soon return and our loved one's readiness to meet Him. A renewal of child-like trust in the power, providence, and promises of God that results in a return of the Holy Spirit in all His Christ-uplifting, life-changing, miracle-working glory to the church. The experience is Pentecost II. The time is the time of the latter rain—and that time could be *now*.

Please don't tune me out. I want to speak from my heart here. (If we were sitting across the kitchen table from each other, I'd lower my voice to get your full attention.) Don't let the term "Pentecost" cause your deodorant to fail. We've been afraid of the Holy Spirit too long. Too easily scared off by images of people rolling on the floor, shaking uncontrollably, and babbling unintelligible sounds. We've associated the *experience* of the Holy Spirit with the *excesses* of emotionalism for so long, that we've fled in the opposite direction and settled for the *theoretical knowledge* of the Holy Spirit instead.

We've been afraid of the Holy Spirit too long.

Bible scholar Gordon Fee states, "The element of spirituality lacking in the contemporary church is the realization that heaven (not as a place but as a promised time) has come to earth in the person of the Spirit. Because of this 'Spirit invasion,' the church should be living out a heavenly life in the here and now. The church of today, however, has bought into the culture's values, which has blurred our understanding of what Paul says about the Holy Spirit."

"Blurred understanding" is putting it mildly for some of us. We've all but tamed the Spirit and capped the wells of salvation that would abundantly supply the water of life our thirsty souls crave. A few years back, a woman writing a letter to the editor of the *Adventist Review* lamented this lack of vision among us. "I'm afraid," she wrote, "we got lost somewhere on our way from Egypt to Canaan and we've been just wandering in circles in the desert."

Like the children of Israel before us, we have explored, sampled, walked through, investigated, observed, and gathered data on revival. *But we've failed to possess the promise!* Consequently, we remain restless wanderers in a desert of dry formalism and monotonous orthodoxy. Our bloated carcasses don't litter a Judean wilderness today. Instead, they waste away on the pews of churches that are often as devoid of the power of God as a tomb is devoid of life!

May I get personal here and speak freely? I want to ask some penetrating questions and I want you to take some time and really think about your answers. What is life like for you in Los Angeles, California; or Vancouver, Washington; or Augusta, Georgia; or Sand Point, Idaho or White Plains; New York, or wherever you call home? What is it like to be in your skin today? What is the condition of your relationships? Your marriage? How are you getting along with your children? How's your health? What is the atmosphere of your home? When was the last time you read the Bible with relish? When was the last time you felt your heart burning within you as you listened to the Word of God preached? How is your relationship with God?

Your career. Is it all you hoped it would be? Your possessions. Your home, cars, clothes, computer or stereo equipment, etc. Are they providing a sense of personal delight and spiritual fulfillment? Your pace of life. Is it rational, balanced, and sane, or has it become a vicious taskmaster that drains the life force from your body leaving you empty?

What is it like to be you tonight? What has your faith become? Is it vibrant, growing? Are you getting deeper with God? Less superficial? Or has growth stopped? Have you lost your first love? Has habit replaced passion? Duty substituted for delight? Routine replaced romance?

While I was typing these words on my laptop computer, the phone rang. The voice belonged to a friend of mine from Los Angeles. She sounded tense and when I asked how she was doing, she replied, "A D-minus." When I probed further, she said nothing in her life was going right. "I've gotten far away from God and I can feel the results of my distance. I have hatred towards those I work with, I've fallen into destructive health habits, and I've been crying my eyes out. I want to get close to Him again."

I don't know where this book finds you today, but God wants to take you to a better place. He wants to embrace you in His arms and restore your soul. He wants you to know that He's real and can give you renewed purpose and joy beyond measure. Will you go with Him?

You know what? There are some things I'm tired of reading about. Some things I don't care to hear second hand. During the Atlanta Olympics, I enjoyed watching the Americans win the gold. I read the recap of the previous day's heroics with relish. For two weeks, I lived vicariously through the "Dream Team," the "Magnificent Seven," and all the other outstanding young men and women who had dedicated their lives to being the best in the world.

I know I'll never be an Olympian. In the arena of world-class sports, I'm content to watch others excel from the sidelines of my living room. But the manifest glory of God is something altogether different. I want a part of that action. I'm not content to merely read about the miracles happening in other people's lives. I'm not satisfied with hearing reports of what the Holy Spirit is doing in eastern Europe, or Russia, or Tanzania. I want to see God at work in my life, in my marriage, on my job, in the lives of my children, and in my nation. This is one time I'm not content to watch from the sidelines!

You and I must pursue, and possess the "undiscovered country" of revival. And we will possess "the land" by prayer, persistence, and promise.

Listen to what God says you and I can have:

> *" 'No eye has seen, no ear has heard, no mind has conceived what God has prepared for those who love him' but God has revealed it to us by his Spirit" (1 Corinthians 2:9, 10, emphasis added).*

Did you see that? Ours is to be an experience unparalleled in the history of earth. Our eyes are to see what no human eyes have seen; Our ears are to hear what no human ears have heard; We're to experience what hasn't even been imagined in the minds of this world's most brilliant scientists, novelists, or politicians. *You and I are the spiritual Magellans of the twenty-first century, with a destination that's not on the distant shores of a new continent but within the veil of the Holy of Holies!*

The latter rain has been looked forward to as some great future event. As it applies to the church at large, this may be true. But I believe it is our privilege to ask God for the fullness of His Spirit *now*. We may possess Jesus, the sweet evidence of pardoned sin and the assurance of salvation, power for witnessing, and intimacy with the Almighty *right now*!

You and I are the spiritual Magellans of the twenty-first century, with a destination that's not on the distant shores of a new continent but within the veil of the Holy of Holies!

The final outpouring may still be future. We can and must seek God for it. But a storm is first preceded by scattered showers, and those early drops can fall on you and me. We've been praying for rain, now it's time we bought galoshes.

There is a land yet undiscovered in its fullness, not because it is hidden but because some have stopped looking. Many have found it, but many more must begin the journey to the undiscovered realm of the Spirit. As with the explorers and pioneers of the past, our journey will require courage, vision, determination and fearlessness. But the rewards will be amazing.

The phrase is well worn, but true just the same. The journey of a thousand miles begins with a single step. The first step is to verbalize our heart's desire—to say, "Bring back the glory, Lord! Bring back the glory of who You are and who You created me to be. Bring back Your glory to my prayer life, my witness, to my relationships and to my walk with You!"

And now, are you ready for God's answer? Do you want to know what happens when God's people pray for revival? Can you stand to be blessed? In the words of Caleb, lets "go up and take possession of the [promise], for we can certainly do it."

---

1. Charlie & Dotty Duke, "Walk on the Moon, Walk with the Son," Life Story Cassette, Campus Crusade, Sumas, WA, 1993.
2. David Lavender, *Westward Vision: The Oregon Trail* (New York: McGraw-Hill Book Company, Inc., 1963), 27.
3. Ibid.

Somehow self and not God rules in the holy of holies.
–E. M. Bounds

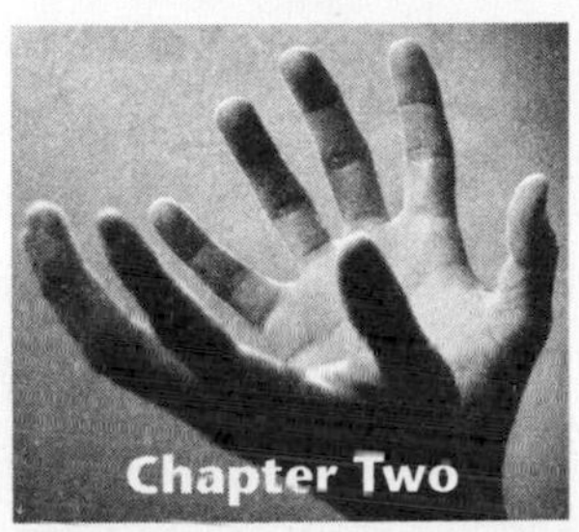

Where's the GLORY?

Mount Carmel. Ranch Apocalypse. Words that trigger strong emotions and even stronger mental pictures of the February 28, 1993 gun battle between armed-to-the-teeth religious fanatics and Rambo-like ATF (Bureau of Alcohol, Tobacco and Firearms) agents who had severely underestimated their targets. I remember seeing the first televised images of agents attempting to enter the Branch Davidian compound through a second-story window. Suddenly, a fierce fire-fight broke out as the agents found themselves trapped on the roof under a hail of bullets that pierced right through the walls. One of the agents was hit as he fled and staggered down a ladder.

When the smoke cleared an undetermined number of Branch Davidians and four ATF agents were dead. Shock and disbelief were etched deeply into the ashen faces of the retreating agents who struggled to carry their dead and wounded comrades to safety. Things had gone terribly wrong. It wasn't supposed to happen that way.

Another confrontation. Another time. There were no cameras present to capture this clash, but the Bible records the incident with these straightforward words: "Now the Israelites went out to fight against the Philistines" (1 Samuel 4:1). With those 10 words, the fourth chapter of Samuel's first book begins. No fluff. No verbiage. Just the facts. Israel went to rumble with some Philistines—their hated rivals.

Next paragraph.

"The Philistines deployed their forces to meet Israel, . . ." (v. 2). Again, no surprises here. Israel had come onto Philistine turf and the Philistines got ready to defend it. But here comes the shocker. "As the battle spread, Israel was defeated by the Philistines, who killed about four thousand of them on the battlefield" (v. 2).

Like the overconfident ATF agents in Waco, who had more swagger than sense, the Israeli army suddenly found themselves "outgunned" and undermanned. Shock and disbelief were etched deeply into the ashen faces of the retreating Israelis who struggled to carry their dead and wounded comrades to safety. Things had gone terribly wrong. Four thousand friends, brothers, and fighting partners lay dead on the field of battle. It wasn't supposed to happen that way.

The forces of Israel returned to camp that night defeated and perplexed, much like our U.S. hockey team in the Nagano Winter Olympic games. The U.S. team was an assemblage of superstars who were supposed to win the gold medal. Analysts and hockey enthusiasts had all but engraved the U.S. team members' names on the gold medals. That is, until the Canadian team sent them home early.

Israel was the "dream team" of their day. Hadn't they been victorious over their enemies before? Hadn't God routed their enemies in miraculous ways? The answer was undeniably Yes. Then what happened? As the soldiers carried in their wounded, the elders of Israel asked " 'Why did the Lord bring defeat upon us today before the Philistines?' "(v. 3)

Why indeed! Poor planning? Arrogance? Carelessness? Whatever the answer was, the debriefing session was cut short. Above the wails and groans of the injured, someone was heard calling for "the closer." Baseball fans will recognize the lingo. The closer is the "stopper"—the star pitcher who can plug the leaks, stop the advance of the enemy, and shut down their ability to score. The closer has a high percentage of wins and is a ball club's secret weapon assuring victory. When the game is on the line, the "closer" comes in.

For Israel the "closer" was the ark of the covenant. This sacred chest had been associated with wonderful revelations of God's truth and power. In former days miraculous victories had been achieved whenever it appeared. It was shadowed by the wings of the golden cherubim, and the unspeakable glory of the Shekinah, the visible symbol of the Most High God, had rested over it in the Holy of Holies.

Now someone suggested: "Let us fetch the ark of the covenant of the Lord out of Shiloh unto us, that, when it cometh among us, it may save us out of the hand of our enemies" (v. 3, KJV).

When the ark first came into camp, a great shout went up from the Israelites—a shout that literally shook the ground. The thunderous sounds of jubilation carried across the battlefield and were heard by the Philistines. " 'What's all this shouting in the Hebrew camp?' " asked the Philistine commanders (v. 6). "Didn't we put a serious hurtin' on those Jews today?" they asked themselves. "Didn't we kill four thousand of their soldiers and watch them flee like cowards in retreat? Why, then, does it sound like they won? Why aren't they filling the air with screams of grief and prayers for deliverance?"

Philistine intelligence quickly learned the reason for Israel's jubilation and spread the word that the ark of the Lord had come into their camp. "A god has come into the camp," they said. "We're in trouble!"

The Philistines may have been heathens, but they knew about the God of the Hebrews. " 'Woe to us! Who will deliver us from the hand of these mighty gods? They are the gods who struck the Egyptians with all kinds of plagues in the desert' " (v. 8).

Waves of panic were about to sweep the Philistine army into a full-fledged retreat, but braver men prevailed. They decided it was better to die facing a god than to surrender and be slaves to the Hebrews. So the two armies clashed again. Israel, this time with the gleaming ark of the covenant, the symbol of Jehovah's presence and power, in their midst. And the Philistines with the cry: "It is a good day to die!" on their lips.

The fighting was fierce—more savage and devastating than before. And when the smoke cleared this time . . . 30,000 Israeli soldiers lay dead (*7.5 times the number lost in the first battle!*), the ark was captured by the enemy, and Eli's two sons, Hophni and Phinehas, were killed while trying to defend it. The defeat of Israel was unexpected and complete.

News of the disastrous battle reached Phinehas's wife who was in the late stages of pregnancy. When she learned that the ark was captured and that her husband, brother-in-law, and father-in-law were dead, she went into labor and gave birth. The labor and the emotional trauma of the day took its toll however, and she began to die. This wife and mother in Israel felt that their last hope as the people of God was gone. With her dying breath she named the child "Ichabod" or "inglorious" saying mournfully, " 'The glory has departed from Israel, for the ark of God has been captured' " (v. 22).

What went wrong?

What caused this defeat of God's people? Why didn't the Lord fight for them as He had before against the Egyptians? Or against the people of Jericho? Why were the people of God—even with the symbol of God's presence among them—so powerless? To find the answers to these questions, we must back up a chapter.

The third chapter of Samuel's first book begins this way: "The boy Samuel ministered before the Lord under Eli. *In those days the word of the Lord was rare; there were not many visions . . . The lamp of God had not yet gone out*" (emphasis added).

Where's the GLORY?

I love the way the Bible slips in subtle statements that reveal profound truths. Notice how the narrator throws out the comment, "The lamp of God had not *yet* gone out." Why was this mentioned? The lamps in the temple service were *never* supposed to go out. The seven-branched golden candlestick, placed on the south side of the Holy Place, was never to go out (see Exodus 27:20, 21). The cups were filled with the best olive oil, symbolic of the Holy Spirit, and the high priest adjusted the lamps morning and evening at the time of placing incense on the altar.[1]

By stating that the lamp had not "yet" gone out, the narrator is letting us know that Israel's spiritual fidelity and zeal for God was at a dangerously low ebb. Evidence of this low spiritual state is seen the earlier statement: "In those days the word of the Lord was rare " or "scarce."

In the days when Eli was high priest in Israel, inspired messages from God were at an all-time low and as a result, "there were not many visions." The people weren't seeing God! The temple was still standing, priests were still administering their duties, the daily round of religious activities was still a part of life for the Israelites, but there was no life! No divine revelation of God. There existed that deplorable situation described by A.W. Tozer when he said, "It is a solemn thing, and no small scandal in the Kingdom, to see God's children starving while actually seated at the Father's table" [2].

How like today! Though Bibles are everywhere (more than 300 translations of the entire Bible exist today—one even in *Pig Latin!*), knowledge of God's Word is rare, even in the lives of many Christians. A 1991 Gallup poll revealed that despite the widespread and continuing popularity of religion, there is "a glaring lack of knowledge about the Bible, basic doctrines, and the traditions of one's own church." This lack of basic Bible knowledge results in inconsistencies and overlapping of beliefs. "People tend to choose the items of belief that best suit them. Reginald Bibby, Canadian sociologist, calls this 'religion a la carte.' Substantial proportions of traditional Christians, for example, subscribe

2—B.B.G.

to non-Christian beliefs and practices, such as reincarnation, channeling, astrology, and fortune telling."[3]

Why this appalling superficiality of faith and lack of knowledge when Bibles are in abundance? Because we're not taking the time to read the Bibles we have. At the gerbil-like pace we live our lives today, if it's not processed into bite-sized morsels that we can consume on the run, we don't have time for it. And that includes the Word of God. This need for speed impacts all aspects of life, not just the religious.

As we gobble and gallop, the Word of God becomes "rare" in our lives.

According to a story in *USA Today*, breakfast is out and "deskfast" is *in*. Our lifestyles have become so mobile that eating cereal in a bowl has given way to toaster-friendly convenience foods that time-poor commuters can gobble at work or in their cars. Soon microwaves will be optional equipment in many makes of automobiles![4]

As we gobble and gallop, the Word of God becomes "rare" in our lives. We manage a surface knowledge of the things of God, but we begin to lose the understanding of the power and promises contained in the Word. Consequently, we too, like the Israelites in Eli's day, suffer from a lack of **VISION**. We're not seeing the Lord. And how do I know that? It's simple: When people see the Lord, their lives are changed.

- When Moses saw the Lord at the burning bush, He removed his shoes. He responded in **reverence** (see Exodus 3:5).
- When Isaiah saw the Lord high and exalted, he immediately **confessed** his sins (see Isaiah 6:1-5).
- When Saul, after being knocked from his horse, saw the Lord on

the road to Damascus, he responded by offering **submission and service.** "Lord, what wilt thou have me to do?" (Acts 9:6, KJV).

In Eli's day there was no reverence, no confession, and no spirit of submission and service. Why? Because God's Word was rare. The people weren't seeing God.

Prayerlessness a factor

The author of the book, *The Kneeling Christian,* makes it clear that *"we cannot get a vision of God unless we pray. And where there is no vision* [no divine revelation of God] *the soul perishes"*[5]

The lack of visions of God must have meant that there weren't many people praying! Again, how like today! People, even church people, are too busy, too tired, too bored, too distracted to pray. Consequently, we grope in darkness, trying to find our way with a match when we've been given the light of the world.

Israel was defeated before the Philistines because she had ignored her God. Their religion had fallen into a mere superstition. They did not realize that theirs was an in-name-only faith that had lost its power to prevail with God. The ark, and the commandments it contained, *was not a part of Israel's daily experience.* Lacking a present-day experience with the Almighty, they recalled stories from their fathers and grandfathers of what God had *done* for Israel in the past. But the experience of their forefathers was not enough. It wasn't enough for them and it isn't enough for us today. It was C. William Fletcher who said, "It is not enough for any generation to be told about the great revivals of the past. There must be a fresh baptism with fire for the sons and daughters, and the atmosphere of revival must prevail in every new day until the Son of Man shall come."[6]

We simply cannot survive spiritually on what *used* to be, or on Grandma's walk with God. I've been to William Miller's farm in New York. I've walked through the maple grove where he wrestled with God about his call to preach, and stood behind the simple wooden lectern in the nearby Miller chapel. I've got the photograph to prove it! But for all its history and nostalgia, Millerism isn't there today.

A few years ago, while leading out in a prayer conference in Memphis, Tennessee, I visited the famed Lorraine Motel where Martin Luther King, Jr. was assassinated. As I approached the motel that now houses the National Civil Rights Museum, traffic sounds faded and the air became very still. I stood transfixed looking up at the large wreathe of white and red flowers fastened to the balcony railing just outside of room 306 where the gilded tongue of Dr. King was silenced by an assassin's bullet on April 4, 1968. From inside the museum, the tour concludes with a viewing inside room 306 where King spent his last hours and ate a final meal with his closest companions. A glass wall allows tourists to view the room where historians have left things untouched–bed unmade, dirty dishes stacked on room service trays–just as King and friends had left them.

With a recording of Mahalia Jackson singing "Precious Lord, Take My Hand," over the sound system, I looked out onto the balcony and saw the spot I had seen so many times in history books. The scene of a fallen Dr. King with three or four companions frantically pointing towards the spot where the shots had originated–an old hotel that I could clearly see through the naked branches of a large tree just across the street. And as I stood there looking out from almost the same vantage point that Dr. King had nearly 30 years earlier, I was moved.

If all we do is make monuments to heroes and immortalize the great revivals of the past, we make the same mistake Israel did.

But for all that he meant to the Civil Rights movement and for all the inspiration that being in that spot generated within me, Martin Luther King, Jr. was not there. His dream lives on, but the vitality and strength of that dream rests in the hands of people like you and me who live it out today.

If all we do is make monuments to heroes and immortalize the great revivals of the past, we make the same mistake Israel did in relying on bygone experiences to pull them through their current crisis. The children of Israel under Eli's spiritual leadership, thought that the form of godliness would save them. They couldn't have been more wrong.

> *When they looked upon the ark, and did not associate it with God, nor honor His revealed will by obedience to His law, it could avail them little more than a common box . . . It was not enough that the ark and the sanctuary were in the midst of Israel. It was not enough that the priests offered sacrifices, and that the people were called the children of God. The Lord does not regard the request of those who cherish iniquity in the heart.*[7]

It was like the now classic "Where's the Beef?" advertising campaign from the 80s for Wendy's hamburgers. A little old lady named Gladys kept trying to find a hamburger that wasn't all bun and little meat. Her complaint, "Where's the beef?" could have been leveled against ancient Israel. The Israelites had all form and no substance. They had the ark, but no Shekinah. The box, but no glory. God had "left the building" and they didn't even know it!

The symptoms of lost glory stretch to our day as well. I received the following e-mail entitled "Progress?" that accurately depicts the shallowness of our times. The author of this piece is, as far as I can tell, unknown.

> *Progress?*
>
> *We have taller buildings, but shorter tempers; wider freeways, but narrower viewpoints; we spend more, but have less; we buy more,*

but enjoy it less.

We have bigger houses and smaller families; more conveniences, but less time; we have more degrees, but less common sense; more knowledge, but less judgment; more experts, but more problems; more medicine, but less wellness.

We spend too recklessly, laugh too little, drive too fast, get too angry too quickly, stay up too late, get up too tired, read too seldom, watch TV too much, and pray too seldom.

We have multiplied our possessions, but reduced our values. We talk too much, love too seldom and lie too often.

We've learned how to make a living, but not a life; we've added years to life, not life to years. We've been all the way to the moon and back, but have trouble crossing the street to meet the new neighbor.

We've conquered outer space, but not inner space; we've done larger things, but not better things; we've cleaned up the air, but polluted the soul; we've split the atom, but not our prejudice; we write more, but learn less; plan more, but accomplish less.

We've learned to rush, but not to wait; we have higher incomes; but lower morals; more food but less appeasement; more acquaintances, but fewer friends; more effort but less success.

We build more computers to hold more information, to produce more copies than ever, but have less communication; we've become long on quantity, but short on quality.

These are the times of fast foods and slow digestion; tall men and short character; steep profits, and shallow relationships. These are the times of world peace, but domestic warfare; more leisure and less fun; more kinds of food, but less nutrition.

These are days of two incomes, but more divorce; of fancier houses, but broken homes.

These are days of quick trips, disposable diapers, throwaway morality, one-night stands, overweight bodies, and pills that do everything from cheer, to quiet, to kill.

It is a time when there is much in the show window, and nothing in the stockroom.

Though it was uttered some 3,100 years ago, the one word that best describes the essence of our times would have to be "Ichabod"—the glory is departed.

The loss of God's glory is not only evident in the secular world. This would surprise no one. But what is shocking and must be confronted is the apparent loss of God's glory in the church of Christ! And this is why Ellen White said "A revival of true godliness among us is the greatest and most urgent of all our needs."[8]

What is Revival?

Revival is defined many ways. The Bible defines it by its results: "Revive us, and we will call on your name" (Psalm 80:18). The implication is that revival produces a people willing to call on the name of the Lord. It produces a spirit of prayer. Evangelist Richard Owen Roberts defines revival: "the reentry of [Christ's] manifest presence." David Bryant, chairman of America's National Prayer Committee and president of Concerts of Prayer International, says "It is Christ showing up in an extraordinarily powerful new way, to significantly overthrow the status quo and establish the claims of His kingdom afresh."[9]

One of my favorite definitions is from D. M. Panton: "the inrush of the Spirit into the body that threatens to become a corpse." In my book, *If My People Pray*, I said that what water and fertilizer are to the nutrient-poor, thirsty soil, revival is to the Spirit-poor, thirsty members of God's church.[10] Revival is a resurrection from near spiritual death. It is the recapturing of our first love. It is the church loving God more than it loves itself.

Oh! How we need revival today!

When is revival needed?

But what is the evidence that we need revival? What conditions exist among God's people that prove we are in need of a return of His glory? Charles Finney, the great revival preacher of the early nineteenth century identified seven spiritual indicators that revival is needed. I'll paraphrase them:

1. *When we don't love each other.* I had a pastor of a small church tell me that something was desperately wrong in his congregation. "We're losing members," he said. "And most of our folk run into these missing members in town all the time, but no one seems to care. No one wants to go after these people." How can we love the "lost" when we can't even love each other?

I remember receiving a rather biting, accusatory e-mail at work from a "brother" who had a beef against the Pacific Press where I work. I normally would have ignored such a letter. (If we responded to every critical letter we receive, we'd never get any work done!) But this one was so nasty, I couldn't let it go. I wrote back to the person and told him that even if he was right and we were guilty of the things he was accusing us of, what made him think that he was justified in attacking his brethren in the spirit of Satan rather than in the Spirit of Christ? Oh the things we do to each other in the name of being "right!"

How long will we endure those individuals among us who have established a long and destructive pattern of devouring pastors and dividing churches? We will rightly censor or disfellowship a member for committing adultery—a sin that is often confined to the parties involved—and leave undisciplined the church board bully who runs roughshod over the pastor and crushes the initiative and spirit of younger members under the weight of their over-inflated egos. These power mongers are self-proclaimed vigilantes of righteousness who leave a trail of brokenness, divisiveness, and hurt in their wake. How long will we allow this to continue?

2. *When dissension, jealousy, and gossip reign supreme in the churches.*

These are just more symptoms of a lack of love. It was Thomas Sine who said, "In the absence of a big dream, pettiness prevails." When our people aren't being inspired to pursue great things for God, pettiness wins the day. We start beating each other up and revealing our desperate need for revival.

3. *When we start getting comfortable with "another kingdom."* By this I mean the church begins to look, act, think, and sound like the world around us. We lose our distinctiveness as God's people and it becomes harder to tell any great difference between Christians and non-Christians. Increasingly we read the same novels, rent the same videos, attend the same concerts, and go to the same places of amusement. Our comfort level with the other kingdom is growing, not diminishing.

4. *When our members fall into gross and scandalous sins.* I heard recently of a number of pastors who were engaged in an illegal pyramid scheme. Are these but echoes to the past when Eli's sons corrupted the priesthood and broke the law so they could profit? (See 1 Samuel 2:12-25.) "When such things are taking place as give the enemies of religion an occasion for reproach, it is time to ask of God: 'What will become of Thy great Name?' "[11]

5. *When there is a spirit of controversy in the church.* Constant bickering and fighting over worship styles, music, and non-essential doctrines indicate the need for revival.

6. *When the church becomes powerless in the face of evil.* Because we're too busy fighting with each other and trying to be as much like the world as possible, evil progresses. Like Nero, we fiddle while the world burns!

Like Nero, we fiddle while the world burns!

---

7. *When sinners are careless and stupid, Christians should shake themselves.* We live in a society that is increasingly shockproof to sin and, through the

new cultural permissiveness, is systematically dismantling the Word of God. Right and wrong are becoming archaic concepts. On a recent flight from Chicago to San Francisco, I was reading a special section of *USA Today* about how television is sinking to new lows. Long gone are the days when showing a roll of toilet paper in a commercial was considered taboo. Today, homosexual acts, nudity, references to male anatomy, and even masturbation, are brazenly scripted into today's hottest TV story lines. Responding to the question of the historic ramifications this lowering standard will have on television, producer Chris Thompson, who developed the show *Action* on the Fox Network, said, "Ultimately, at the very bottom line, it's not about what significance it had on the scheme of television. It's 'Was it funny? Are you laughing?' "[12]

"The world has lost the power to blush over its vice; the church has lost her power to weep over it."

Never mind the morals and values that are in direct conflict with the revealed will of God in His Word. *Was it funny!* A.W. Tozer was right in saying, "America is laughing her way to hell." And while she laughs, does the church laugh with her? Leonard Ravenhill looks the church dead in the eye and sighs, "The world has lost the power to blush over its vice; the church has lost her power to weep over it." We need a revival to wake us up to the soul carnage going on all around us.

Hope in the darkness

Now we return to that cryptic statement by the narrator in 1 Samuel 3:3, "The lamp of God had not yet gone out." The first thing this statement reveals, as we've seen, is that the spiritual condition of the people was poor. But the second message is one of hope. *The lamp of God still flickered.*

True, the light of God's revealed presence was dim and growing dimmer by the minute, but the flame was not yet extinguished. Why not? Because somebody *was* praying!

Who was that somebody? Hannah, of course. Little did she realize that her prayers for a son would birth a revival in Israel.

Matthew Henry said, "Whenever God intends great mercy for His people, it is He, first of all, who sets them a praying." God wanted a revival in Israel. He wanted "a faithful priest," who would do according to what was in God's heart and mind (see 1 Samuel 2:35). And so, in solving Hannah's problem, God solved His own. Many years later when He needed a man to stand in the gap for Israel, He had one in the prophet Samuel.

Hannah's struggles were a reflection of Israel's in miniature. Hannah was barren—probably the worst thing that could happen to a woman in the ancient world, besides being a widow. She begged God to remove the shame of her barrenness and give her a son. Her prayers were agonizing episodes of weeping and fasting (see 1 Samuel 1:7). Though her husband loved her the way she was, Hannah would not be consoled in her desire to bear a child. God heard the prayers of one woman and, once again, He had a channel through whom He could communicate with His people.

And this is why you and I can have hope. *God must intend to send revival to modern Israel, because He's setting His people to praying.* Since writing *If My People Pray* in 1995, I have witnessed a growing hunger for prayer on the part of God's people. Christians are getting tired of playing church. They are growing restless with business as usual and want "the beef" of an authentic walk with God. Through e-mails, phone calls, and face-to-face dialogue with church members and pastors across the country, I'm hearing a Hannah-like desire for revival not unlike this description from James Burns:

> *Preceding revivals, there often seems to be a widespread spirit of dissatisfaction among those God is preparing for what He is about to*

do. The heart of man begins to cry out for God, for spiritual certainties, for fresh visions. From a faint desire this multiplies as it widens, until it becomes a vast human need; until in its urgency it seems to beat with violence at the very gates of heaven.[13]

How about it? Are you hungry? As you read these words is your heart bursting within you to see the Lord return in new glory to your life, to your home, to your church? Can you sense within a growing urge to "beat with violence at the very gates of heaven" for the promised outpouring of the Holy Spirit?

Do you wish a revival? Will you have one? If God should ask you this moment, by an audible voice from heaven, "Do you want a revival?" would you dare to say: "Yes?" If He were to ask: "Are you willing to make the sacrifices?" would you answer: "Yes?" And if He said: "When shall it begin?" would you answer: "Let it begin to-night—let it begin here—let it begin in my heart NOW"?[14]

I'm not ashamed to tell you that even as I type these heart-searching questions posed by Charles Finney, I'm shaking inside. I do not take them lightly. I shrink before the implications of saying Yes. And yet what else can I do? The alternative is to stay dead—to be forever "Ichabod." God, help us to say Yes to You and bring back the glory!

In the following chapters, we'll look at the steps God wants us to take for a return of His glory in our lives. The steps aren't always going to be smooth, but the Father knows the way.

---

1. *Seventh-day Adventist Bible Commentary* (Washington, D.C.: Review and Herald Publishing Association, 1976), 2:466.
2. A.W. Tozer, *The Pursuit of God* (Camp Hill, Penn.: Christian Publications, Inc., 1982), 9.
3. George Gallup, Jr., *Poll Releases*, April 2, 1999: "Easter Draws Americans Back to Church"

Internet: www.gallup.com/poll/releases/pr990402b.asp
4. Bruce Horovitz, "Need for speed drives cereal killer," *USA Today*, January 22, 1999, p. 2B.
5. *The Kneeling Christian* (Grand Rapids: Zondervan Publishing House, 1986), 53.
6. C. William Fischer, *It's Revival We Need!* (Kansas City: Nazarene Publishing House, 1968), 12.
7. Ellen G. White, *Patriarchs and Prophets*, p. 584.
8. Ellen G. White, *Selected Messages,* book 1, p. 121
9. David Bryant, "What Are You Praying Toward?" *Pray!* Magazine, Jan/Feb 1998, p. 12.
10. Randy Maxwell, *If My People Pray*, (Nampa, Id.: Pacific Press Publishing Association, 1995), 155.
11. Charles Finney, *Revivals of Religion*(Westwood, NJ: Fleming H. Revell Company, 1965), 18.
12. Gary Lewis, "TV Turns On," *USA Today*, Section E, September 24, 1999.
13. Colin Whittaker, *Great Revivals*, (London: Marshall Pickering, 1984 and 1999), 68.
14. Charles Finney, *Revivals of Religion*, p. 34

Groanings which cannot be uttered
are often prayers which cannot be refused.
–C.H. Spurgeon

We are wondering why God does not move;
He is wondering why we do not break!
–Leonard Ravenhill

"Therefore also now, saith the Lord, turn ye even to me with all your heart, and with fasting, and with weeping, and with mourning."
–Joel 2:12, KJV

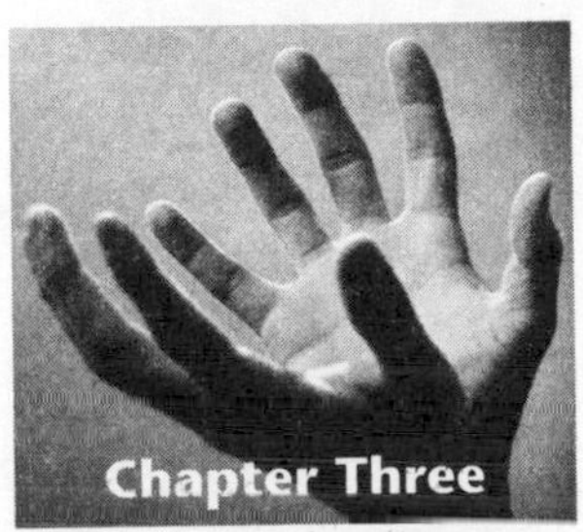

The GLORY of Brokenness

My wife is one of ten million Americans who suffer from a painful condition known as Dry Eye Syndrome. People who have dry eyes simply don't make enough tears. And if *quantity* of tears isn't the problem, a decline in the *quality* of tears can also cause the condition. Either way, dry eye hurts, as Suzette can readily testify. When her allergies are flaring up, she often complains that her eyes feel like someone has scratched them with sandpaper, and without eye washes and artificial tears, the irritation can lead to scarring or ulceration of the cornea, and ultimately a loss of vision.

Some of the warning signs of Dry Eye Syndrome are:

- an inability to cry under emotional stress
- decreased tolerance of contact lenses
- sensitivity to light causing severe eye pain or diminished vision.

But as painful as Dry Eye Syndrome is physically, *spiritual* dry eyes are even worse. When our eyes don't water at the sight of empty pews and the empty hearts of those who should be "filled with the Holy Spirit," we suffer from spiritual Dry Eye Syndrome. When the icy coldness of formality creeps into our prayer life and the chronic lack of passion in our walk with God doesn't cause us to weep in despair, we have "Dry Eye Syndrome." When we can sing "We Have This Hope" dry eyed while empty baptistries stare back at us, a stark reminder of how little impact that "hope" is making on those living within the shadow of our churches, we've got Dry Eye Syndrome.

And as we shake our heads in perplexity and wonder "why *God* does not move; He is wondering why *we* do not break! We wish *He* would bend low; He wishes *we* would break down."[1]

My friends, revival eludes us because we are struggling for all we're worth to appear spiritually healthy and whole, while the Lord wants us weak and broken in His presence. This is where revival begins—at the altar of brokenness.

Brokenness, key to revival

I remember the morning I broke before God. I was tired. The kind of tired that goes all the way to the bone. I had stayed up late too many nights and had started too many days without connecting with the Lord in any kind of meaningful way. Here I was conducting prayer conferences and telling others about the importance of prayer and I was missing out myself. School pressures, work pressures, family and church responsibilities, plus the nagging fear that having preached to others, I would end up a "castaway," drove me to my knees that morning. My wife was at my side that day. In addition to everything else, we were both feeling the effects of a prolonged season of spiritual dryness. Nothing we did brought a sense of joy or refreshment. All was dry, flat, and uninspired.

When I began praying that day, I had no intention of crying. Tears were not on my agenda. But the more I talked to God, the more I felt my need of Him. Soon I began to honestly express my weariness, my out-of-control-ness. I saw how empty and shallow I was and the sight sickened me. Then something within me broke. Out of the depths of my arid, depleted spirit came forth a cry of "O God, I need You so much!" Quite unexpectedly I began to sob and tears of desire tumbled from my eyes.

Suzette, who had been praying beside me, enfolded me in her arms and the cry of my heart opened the floodgates of her heart as well. We held each other allowing the Holy Spirit to minister to our brokenness through cleansing tears of conviction, confession, and repentance. We had come to the end of ourselves and that is exactly what God had been waiting for.

This personal revelation is not shared to make you think we are super-spiritual or anything like that. Just the opposite! We were running on empty. We were out of sync with God and finally vomited up the barrenness of our souls. We needed to be broken that morning and believe me *we need it still today!*

Brokenness. What a backwards concept for today's Christian! What an old-fashioned foreign word to most of us. But remember this: *There can be no Pentecost without Calvary!* No revival without brokenness.

Joel 2:28, 29 is a favorite text to dwell on and quote when painting an inspiring picture of what God will do when He pours out His Spirit. Who isn't excited when they read these prophetic words: " 'And afterward, I will pour out my Spirit on all people. Your sons and daughters will prophesy, your old men will dream dreams, your young men will see visions. Even on my servants, both men and women, I will pour out my Spirit in those days' "?

The Lord moving in power among His people! A return of the glory of His presence and His wonders! Our heart yearns for these. And we may have all of it. It is surely promised. But we cannot ignore the *means* God requires us to use to secure the blessing. What are those means? Brokenness.

Notice this revival promise begins with the words "And afterward . . ." After what? Something obviously comes first, before the Lord pours out

His Spirit on all people. Back up and look at verses 12-17 for the answer:

> *"Even now," declares the Lord, "return to me with all your heart, with fasting and weeping and mourning." Rend your heart and not your garments. Return to the Lord your God, for he is gracious and compassionate, slow to anger and abounding in love, and he relents from sending calamity . . . Blow the trumpet in Zion, declare a holy fast, call a sacred assembly. Gather the people, consecrate the assembly; bring together the elders, gather the children, those nursing at the breast. Let the bridegroom leave his room and the bride her chamber. Let the priests, who minister before the Lord, weep between the temple porch and the altar. Let them say, "Spare your people, O Lord. Do not make your inheritance an object of scorn, a byword among the nations. Why should they say among the peoples, 'Where is their God?' "*

There it is! The first step in revival. A call to "return" to God with all our hearts. A call to self-denial. A call to tears. A call to repentance. Are you disappointed? Is the thought of self-denial and soul-grief distasteful to you? I'll be honest, it is to me! The cross is always distasteful. It is "a stumbling block to Jews and foolishness to Gentiles" (1 Corinthians 1:23). It is a place where my pride gets put to death, and pride doesn't go without a fight! "This is why," writes James Burns, "a revival has ever been unpopular with large numbers within the church. Because it says nothing to them of power such as they have learned to love, or of ease, or of success; it accuses them of sin, it tells them that they are dead, it calls them to awake, to renounce the world, and to follow Christ."[2]

If we attempt to bypass the "rent heart," we cannot have the outpouring of God's Spirit promised "afterward." One is the means, the other the ends. Skip the method, lose the results.

The sacred assembly

I've often wondered what this would look like in our day. Joel presents a picture of the utmost solemnity. Everyone is present. No one—not nursing child, newlymarried couples, senior citizens, priests—no one is missing. Vacations have been canceled, Sabbath picnics postponed. Everyone is gathered before the Lord to rend their hearts and seek the return of His glory among them. What would this type of "sacred assembly" look like today? Would we come to church as we normally do and look for a bulletin? Would we find "Weeping and mourning service" listed just beneath "Tithes and offering" or "Garden of Prayer" on the program? Would we come in our usual Sabbath dress, or would we be handed burlap vests from grim-faced greeters when we entered the sanctuary? (For many churches, the grim-faced greeters would be nothing new!) Would there be a sermon or a season of prayer or silence as individuals wrestled with God privately over their Dry Eye Syndrome? What would the visitors think? Would our young people be totally turned off? Could we get our hearts properly "rent" before noon? (That's as long as many can give the Lord. After 12:00, it's "our" time again.)

I'm not sure what the answer is, but I think it's worth our time to think and talk about it. As I said in the introduction of this book, the world is approaching its spiritual midnight but the church of Christ is living as if it's only 9:30! We simply cannot continue business as usual in our churches. Comfort cannot continue to be our first priority. Our clothing, our degrees, our sophistication, our order of service, our building, our pews, our carpeting, our wealth, our positions—none of that stuff impresses God! What does impress Him? "The sacrifices of God are a broken spirit; a broken and contrite heart, O God, you will not despise" (Psalm 51:17).

The sacred assembly must be called if we're serious about revival*. In our services, we've got to give God time to get through to our hard hearts. Preachers, maybe you could shorten the message so our people could pray more. Or perhaps we could give less time to announcements so we could give more time to intercession. Get a group of people together from your church and talk to God about it. Ask Him to show you how to call a sacred assembly in your church. In the meantime, lets begin the process individually by crying out to the Lord for the attitude of brokenness. And it starts with an admission of need.

Admit how much we need healing.

Ellen White, on page 95 of *Steps to* Christ, writes: "There are certain conditions upon which we may expect that God will hear and answer our prayers. One of the first of these is that we feel our need of help from Him." God Himself affirmed this principle of humility when He spoke this promise through the prophet Isaiah: "I will pour water upon him that is thirsty, and floods upon the dry ground" (Isaiah 44:3, KJV).

Remember this: God is attracted to weakness. He can't resist the humble prayers of His people who cry out to Him for help. It is the thirsty who get the water; the "dry ground" that receives "floods."

In the previous chapter we considered Hannah. Hannah was the picture of brokenness. She knew she was barren. She felt the shame of it and begged God to remove it from her. Laodicea, the lukewarm church that our era is epitomized by, is also barren, but doesn't know it! Hannah felt the shame of being unable to reproduce a child. Laodicea is unable to reproduce the character of Christ, but feels no shame. Admits no need.

This reminds me of an incident that happened with my youngest daughter one summer day when she was just a baby. I had just put the car in the garage after giving it a long-overdue bath. I was watering the flowers in front of the house when suddenly I became aware of the happy sounds of the neighborhood ice cream truck. The brightly-painted vehicle rounded the corner near my home and stopped by the curb in front of the house next door. Eager children—some with parents in tow—came bounding past my property to stand in line for the icy treats. I smiled watching them, knowing how my own children loved ice cream and wondered where they were.

Suddenly, I noticed that the children were looking away from the ice cream vendor towards me. They had these big, goofy grins on their faces and some were chuckling. Well, I quickly verified that there was nothing wrong with me. I then followed their gaze to my still-open garage where, to my horror (not hers) stood two-year-old Danielle, in all her natural-born splendor, arms upraised and squealing, "Ice cream, ice cream. Daddy, I want ice cream."

Nakedness of a baby is cute.
Spiritual nakedness of the church of Christ is cause for tears.

I dropped the garden hose and covered the distance between us in a single bound. Like a defensive back pouncing on a fumbled football, I scooped Dani up in my arms and disappeared into the house. I was embarrassed for her and moved as quickly as I could to cover her shame and shield her from onlookers. Danielle, on the other hand, was wondering what all the fuss was about. She didn't know she was naked. Didn't care. All she wanted was ice cream. The next thing she knew, she was being air-lifted back into the house by this bug-eyed maniac who was ranting to everyone and no one in particular, *"Who's watching the baby? Didn't anybody know she was outside with no clothes on?"*

Nakedness of a baby is cute. Spiritual nakedness of the church of Christ is cause for tears.

Remember the children's story, "The Emperor's New Clothes?" The Emperor was deceived into thinking he was wearing exquisite garments that only the wise could see. He was naked as a jaybird, but because none of his subjects wanted to appear foolish, they pretended to see what wasn't there. Finally a little boy told the truth and the emperor, though terribly embarrassed, put on some clothes and covered his shame. Who will tell the truth to the church today?

Back in the 1960s, a Christian leader in India by the name of Bakht Singh saw the crying need of his American brethren and told the "emperor" the truth in a magazine called *Conquest for Christ*:

> *The indigenous churches in India have a great burden for America just now . . . and are praying that God will visit your country with revival . . . You feel sorry for us in India because of our poverty in* **material** *things. We who know the Lord in India feel sorry for you in America because of your* **spiritual** *poverty. We pray that God may give you gold tried in the fire which He had promised to those who know the power of His resurrection . . . . In our churches we spend four or five or six hours in prayer and worship, and frequently our people wait on the Lord in prayer all night, but in America after you have been in church for one hour, you begin to look at your watches. We pray that God may open your eyes to the true meaning of worship . . . . To attract people to meetings, you have a great dependence on posters, on advertising, on promotion, and on the build-up of a human being; in India we have nothing more than the Lord Himself and we find that He is sufficient. Before a Christian meeting in India we never announce who the speaker will be. When the people come, they come to seek the Lord and not a human being or to hear some special favorite speaking to them. We have had as many as 12,000 people come together just to worship the Lord and to have fellowship together. We are praying that the people in America might also come to church with a hunger for God and not merely a hunger to see some form of amusement or hear choirs or the voice of any man.*[3]

Recently, I attended the celebration ceremonies of a respected Christian institution. One of the evening speakers presented a dynamic presentation showing how the stage of human history was being set for the fulfillment of Bible prophecy in regards to a coming religio-political union. The facts were compelling, and the speaker presented them in such a skillful manner as to convince everyone that the great controversy between Christ and Satan was indeed nearing its close. As a Seventh-day Adventist Christian, my heart resonated with the truth of what was being shared and those around me also responded with enthusiasm at the prospect of Jesus' soon return.

Immediately after the presentation, I was called aside by one of the leaders of this organization. With a heavy heart this leader asked me if I would pray for him and his fellow leaders. As the story tumbled out, a misunderstanding had occurred between representatives in two different regions. Heated, even profane words had been exchanged. Several people—fellow workers in the same outstanding cause—were not speaking to each other and now this leader was at a loss as to how to reconcile the offended brethren.

My own heart felt the weight of this man's burden. I was struck with the contrast between the presentation we had just seen moments ago, verifying the nearness of Christ's return, and the battle of wills and pride just revealed through this leader's prayer request. "How can we see the signs of the times and get excited about the Lord's return," I said, "and not see that *we aren't ready for Him?*"

It would appear as if the closer Jesus gets to returning, the further His people get from repenting.

The emperor has no clothes and we need to know the truth! With churches splitting over power issues, pastors becoming entangled in illegal financial schemes, racial prejudice keeping members at arm's length from each other, and endless struggles over positions and control, it would appear as if the closer Jesus gets to returning, the further His people get from repenting. We marvel at how dense the disciples were when, after three and a half years of being with Jesus, they still didn't understand His mission and fought among themselves for supremacy right up until the time of Jesus' arrest. After all they had been through, seen and done, they were still selfish little children. How this must have saddened the heart of Christ!

But these men had only three and half years to know the Savior. The church of Christ has had 2,000! *What's our excuse?* You would think that after two millennia of church going, Bible reading, hymn singing, witness giving, book writing, seminary training, etc., we'd be a little closer to growing up into Christ. You'd think we'd be digesting the "meat" of the Word by now, but we're still nursing at the breast—still tiny "babes in Christ" (see 1 Corinthians 3:1, KJV). Why? Because instead of breaking, many have been faking. Because we've done more hymn singing and debating than we've done people loving and soul searching.

"This is the time," writes Ravenhill, "to blush that we have no shame, the time to weep for our lack of tears, the time to bend low that we have lost the humble touch of servants, the time to groan that we have no burden, the time to be angry with ourselves that we have no anger over the devil's monopoly in this 'end time' hour, the time to chastise ourselves that the world can so easily get along with us and not attempt to chastise us."[4] Oh, that God would open our eyes to our spiritual barrenness and cause us to weep like Hannah to have the shame of our nakedness removed! We have a need today.

Be a servant

Jesus said, "Whoever wants to become great among you must be your servant, and whoever wants to be first must be slave of all. For even the Son of Man did not come to be served, but to serve, and to give his life as a ransom for many" (Mark 10:43-45). Is servanthood on your agenda? Do you always have to be right? Always first? Always applauded? Always the authority on everything? To develop the attitude of brokenness, we must have Christ's servant heart.

"Are you willing," writes Keith Green, "to be a nothing? Are you willing to go anywhere and do anything for Christ? Are you willing to stay right where you are and let the Lord do great things through you, though nobody seems to care or notice at all?"[5]

Serve first, be right second. Put your neighbor's needs and concerns ahead of your need for strokes and attention. Be willing to admit your faults and confess how much self reigns on the throne of your heart.

Be willing to "die" so others can live

Hear Moses say to the Lord, " 'Oh, what a great sin these people have committed! They have made themselves gods of gold. But now, please forgive their sin–but if not, then blot me out of the book you have written' " (Exodus 32:31, 32). Hear the Apostle Paul say: "I have great sorrow and unceasing anguish in my heart. For I could wish that I myself were cursed and cut off from Christ for the sake of my brothers, . . ." (Romans 9:2, 3). And of course, our Lord "did not consider equality with God something to be grasped, but made himself nothing, taking the very nature of a servant, being made in human likeness. And being found in appearance as a man, he humbled himself and became obedient to death–even death on a cross!" (Philippians 2:6-8)

These were all willing to die so that others might live. Are we? Am I? Before you raise your hands to join the ranks of the martyrs, consider how hard it is for many of us to give up our seat in church to a visitor, let alone give our lives to save a brother.

I remember attending a church where I was to speak for Sabbath services. It was a high Sabbath and the church was packed. Seats were hard to find. After the service, my host explained that she had had an unfortunate clash with a member just before church began over some seats she had been saving. My host tried in vain to explain that she was saving seats for some guests—non-Christians who had never been to that church before—that she had personally invited. Instead of the church member being willing to graciously give up the seats for visitors who might hear the gospel for the first time, this person got angry and stormed out of the building!

People with the attitude of brokenness are willing to "lay down their lives" for others. To surrender their "rights" and their positions of power to help lift someone else up. Give up your pew. Give up your anger and your grudge. If a church office stands between you and your brother or sister, *give it up*! To paraphrase Paul, "Do not by [your church office, title, or pew] destroy your brother for whom Christ died" (Romans 14:15).

What would this look like in real life? I'm thinking of a church I've ministered in that suffered a devastating split. After several months, members of the "splinter" group had a change of heart and wanted to rejoin the mother church. You would think this would be cause for rejoicing, right? And for many in the mother church, it would be. But there are those who aren't quite ready to kill the fatted calf. There is concern that these returning ones might want their old church offices back!

Basin theology

What about another scenario? What would happen if the hearts of these "elder brothers" grieved more for the spiritual wellness of their separated brethren than for the potential loss of an office? What if they welcomed their returning brethren with a basin and a towel and offered to humbly wash their feet? What if they looked their "prodigal" brother or sister in the eye and said, "Your return to our family means more than anything, and if it takes getting your old church office back to make you feel welcome and affirmed, I'll gladly step down so you can serve again." That, my friends is "basin theology," and it can only come from a heart that has been broken at the foot of the cross.

Telling the truth

Brokenness and honesty go hand in hand. Keith Anderson, a friend of mine who writes a bi-weekly column in the religion section of the *Idaho Press Tribune* began one of his columns with this prayer:

> *Lord God, I ask for your forgiveness. All this time I have acted as though I was a Christian. I have continued to do things that Christians aren't supposed to do. Forgive me for all of my lies. The biggest lie of all is claiming that I am a Christian. As I take a look at myself, I realize that by your standards, I am not a Christian at all. I pray that you work on my heart. I pray that you work on my attitude. I pray that you teach me priorities.*[6]

It's hard to pray like that. It's hard for me to look in the mirror and say, "You are the man!" Not *"You da man!"* the popularized phrase that I say when I mean to congratulate myself on being the best at something. But the "You-are-the-man" admission of guilt and failure that the prophet Nathan leveled against King David after his sin (see 2 Samuel 12:1-13). Like the old spiritual says, "It's me, it's me, it's *me* O Lord, standin' in the need of prayer."

We've all got to be honest about ourselves with God. As hard as this may be, it's necessary if we want the promise of Joel 2:28, 29 fulfilled in our lives and churches. God has spelled out the way of revival. His means aren't hidden or a mystery. But sometimes we want different things. We want Pentecost without Calvary. We want glory without humility. We want revival on *our* terms, within the confines of *our* schedules. A bloodless coup. A crossless gospel. It's like Wilbur Rees's poem:

> *I would like to buy $3 worth of God please. Not enough to explode my soul or disturb my sleep, but just enough to equal a cup of warm milk, or a snooze in the sunshine. I don't want enough of Him to make me love a black [or a White, Asian, Hispanic] man or pick*

beets with a migrant. I want ecstasy, not transformation. I want the warmth of the womb, not a new birth. I want a pound of the eternal in a paper sack. I would like $3 worth of God.[7]

Can we be honest with God today? Do you truly want revival? In his book, *Brokenness, the Forgotten Factor of Prayer*, Mickey Bonner writes, "His moving will come in only one way. It will not be by great singing, concerts, or music. It will not come by dynamic preaching. It will only happen when men become so broken before God that their only hope is Jesus Christ and His intervention. God moves only through tears of brokenness. Historically, as well as Biblically, we find that man's view of God's Will is seen only through tears. His ways are not our ways."[8]

Don't be discouraged! The way down is the way up! "Those who sow in tears will reap with songs of joy" (Psalm 126:5). Immediately after the "sacred assembly" of repentance in Joel 2:15-17, we have the promises of restoration in verses 18-32. This is what can happen when God's people pray for revival. Who will prove the Lord to be true to His Word? I want to. I confess that I am not broken enough before the Lord , and tears alone are worthless if they don't result in obedience. Tears like these are what E.M. Bounds calls "surface slush." No, no. I want a heart broken and tenderized by the things that break God's heart. Don't you?

---

* If you would like to participate in an online sacred assembly, praying for repentance and revival with brothers and sisters from around the world, visit the author's website at **http://www.tagnet.org/ifmypeoplepray/**

1. Leonard Ravenhill, *Revival Praying* (Minneapolis: Bethany House Publishers, 1962, 1996), 114.
2. C. William Fischer, *It's Revival We Need!* (Kansas City: Nazarene Publishing House, 1968), 12.
3. Leonard Ravenhill, *Revival Praying* (Minneapolis: Bethany House Publishers, 1962 and 1996), 41, 42.
4. Leonard Ravenhill, *Why Revival Tarries* (Minneapolis: Bethany House Publishers, 1997), 65.

5. Keith Green, "Music or Missions?" I couldn't find the original publication where this article appears, though I believe it came from Green's *Last Days* magazine.
6. Keith Anderson, "Fathers of faith paid high price for beliefs," *Idaho Press Tribune*, section C, March 28, 1998.
7. Wilbur Rees, "$3.00 Worth of God," *Improving Your Serve*, by Charles Swindoll (Waco, Tex.: Word Books, 1981), 29.
8. Mickey Bonner, *Brokenness, the Forgotten Factor of Prayer* (Houston: Mickey Bonner Evangelistic Association, 1996), 12.

To the question, "Where is the Lord God of Elijah?"
we answer, "Where He has always been—on the throne!"
But where are the Elijahs of God?
–Leonard Ravenhill

God creates desperation in your heart for a purpose.
Every place of desperation is the door to restoration.
The Bible calls it hunger and thirst.
–Wellington Boone

"The effectual fervent prayer of a righteous man availeth much."
–James 5:16, KJV

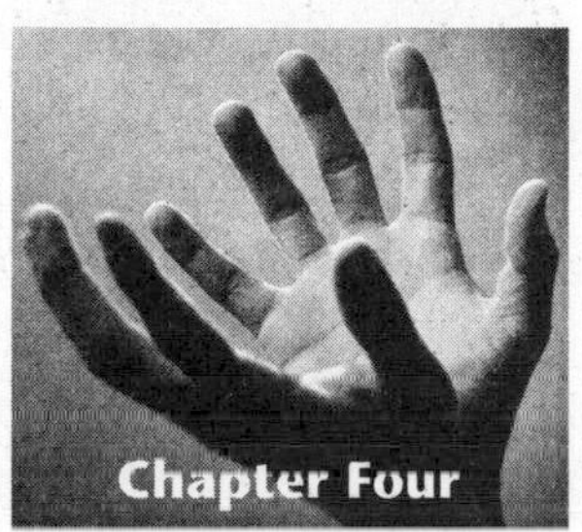

The GLORY of Prevailing Prayer

The grainy black and white photo of a guy in running shoes, doubled over and vomiting, immediately caught my eye. *This is different,* I thought, as I looked through the eight-page NIKE® ad piece, promoting their newest innovation in athletic footwear. How could something so gross be used to sell shoes? There was no way I wasn't going to read the copy captioning such an unattractive picture. As I read, it became clear what NIKE® was up to.

Right after Bob Kempainen qualified for the marathon, he crossed the finish line and puked all over his NIKE® running shoes. We can't tell you how proud we were. Unfortunately, his moment of glory was cut short when the networks took the cameras off him. Why? Did he offend the commercial sponsors? Was it detrimental to the ratings? Was it all just a little too intense and 3-D for the folks at home? TOUGH. If they really want to support athletes, if they really want to be a part of the experience, they can't just turn up for the photo opportunities and the media events, and smile and mug for the cameras. They've got to accept THE WHOLE ENCHILADA. And it's a spitting, cussing, sweating, blister-breaking enchilada, with extra cramps. GET USED TO IT.

I knew then that NIKE® was using this photo to sell more than running shoes. They were selling desire. They were selling heart. They were selling effort, guts, and glory. With this in-your-face ad copy NIKE® was saying, "You want to win? You want to be first across the finish line? You want to achieve your goal? Then it's going to take everything you've got. You may not look pretty getting there, but the prize will be yours and no one can take it away from you."

On another page of the insert, they threw out the challenge:

It's not enough to just want to be the best. You can't just sit around and BS about how much you want it. Show me how much you want it. Stop just 'thinking about it' and 'wondering about it' and 'hoping for it' and actually go out there and get it. Dare to do what it takes to be the best and then, whether you win, lose or collapse on the finish line, at worst, you'll know exactly who you are.

Call me weird. Call me strange, but when I read this insert, I wasn't thinking athletics; I was thinking prayer. I wasn't thinking shoes; I was thinking revival. I was thinking about me, and my commitment to the prize I claim to be running for. I was thinking about my passion (or the lack thereof) for the God I claim to be loving with all my heart, mind and soul. I looked at the photo of the upchucking marathon runner and thought, *He emptied the bucket; gave it everything he had—do I?*

We all know that prayer is the key to revival. In prayer God has given us a mighty weapon—something as great as Himself. But, as Spurgeon said, "we have permitted it to rust." Why? Let's be honest. There are times when prayer is deep and holy and awesome. Prayer can be a cathedral of stars on a summer night or the breath of a newborn baby asleep on its mother's breast. But there are also times when prayer is "a spitting, cussing, sweating, blister-breaking enchilada, with extra cramps." And if we intend to see revival in our lifetimes, we'd better get used to it! This is, as Chuck Swindoll is fond of saying, "no time for wimps!"

Prayer and revival talk is chic right now. It's like the angel craze of recent years that has heaven's messengers on everything from Disney films to soap-on-a-rope. The prayer "movement" is also growing in popularity. People are joining prayer teams and prayer groups, having prayer vigils, and concerts of prayer. I know; I travel the country conducting prayer and revival conferences. Don't get me wrong. I'm thrilled with what I believe is a sovereign move of God to call His people to prayer. The hunger that has been awakened in my heart and in the hearts of so many who crave intimacy with the Almighty is a joy to see.

And yet, if we are to enter into a second Pentecost, if we're to experience the "revival of primitive godliness" that is "our greatest need," we can't "turn off" or turn away when the going gets intense (and things are about to get a lot more intense!) We can't just turn up for the prayer conference "photo opportunities" and smile and go for appearances. Now is the time to "empty the bucket" in prayer and refuse to sit around "thinking about," "wondering about," and "hoping" for revival. It's time to take God at His word, go on the spiritual offensive and claim the blessing He longs to give—Now! "I tell you, *now* is the time of God's favor, *now* is the day of salvation" (2 Corinthians 6:2, emphasis added).

Do you want to get well?

At this point, I can't help but think of the invalid at the pool of Bethesda (see John 5). This was no ordinary pool. From time to time the waters in the pool would move—*on their own!* Local legend had it that an angel of the Lord would come down and stir up the waters. People came from miles around, not just to witness the phenomena, but to be the first to get *in* when the water moved. Folks believed that the first one into the pool after each disturbance of the water would be cured of whatever disease he or she had. And the fact is, many people had been healed this way!

Now this invalid had been at the pool for thirty-eight years. Jesus saw him lying there and asked the man an incredible question: "Do you want to get well?" Jesus can ask some amazing questions! Imagine thirty-eight years of weakness and frailty. Thirty-eight years of not being able to support a family and earn an honest wage for honest labor. Thirty-eight years of relying on the kindness of strangers and of suffering that brand of invisibility that society bequeaths to its elderly, poor, and sick.

" 'Sir,' " the invalid replied, 'I have no one to help me into the pool when the water is stirred. While I am trying to get in, someone else goes down ahead of me' " (v. 7). Thirty-eight years of having healing within his reach only to be disappointed time after time as others got the blessing he so desperately wanted. *Did he want to get well!* The man's answer indicates that he wanted Jesus to know he was trying his best. He wasn't a quitter; he just wasn't fast enough.

"Then Jesus said to him, 'Get up! Pick up your mat and walk.' At once the man was cured; he picked up his mat and walked" (v. 8).

Today, Jesus asks you and me, "Do you want to get well?" He has the right to ask it because, like the invalid, we have been lying in Laodicean paralysis for years! We've had access to the cure all along. It is within our reach, but we have opted instead to think, wonder, and hope for healing. If you really do want to get well, Jesus says, "Get on your knees. Pick up your faith and *pray!"* Or, to use NIKE® lingo: "Just do it!"

The Bible says that, "the prayer of a righteous man is powerful and effective" (James 5:16). I want to take this chapter and the next to look at the role of "powerful and effective" prayer in revival. Charles Finney calls this "prevailing prayer." What are the characteristics of this type of praying and what can we expect as we practice it? What can we learn from the prayer experience of Hannah and the Disciples at Pentecost that will help us obtain the Father's blessing? Let's begin with thirst.

Obey your thirst

Ever been thirsty? I mean, *really* thirsty? Antoine de Saint-Exupéry, the famous French aviator and author, knew real thirst when he and his mechanic crashed their plane and wandered for three days in the burning sands of the Sahara desert. In his book, *Wind, Sand and Stars*, the Frenchman describes his thirst:

> *The wind that shrivels up a man in nineteen hours was now blowing out of the west. My gullet was not yet shut, but it was hard and painful and I could feel that there was a rasp in it. Soon that cough would begin that I had been told about and was now expecting. My tongue was becoming a nuisance. But most serious of all, I was beginning to see shining spots before my eyes. When those spots changed into flames, I should simply lie down . . . . Thirsty I was, yes, and it seemed to me that I was suffering less from thirst itself than from the effects of thirst. Gullet hard. Tongue like plaster-of-Paris. A rasping in the throat. A horrible taste in the mouth . . . . Thirst had become more and more a disease and less and less a craving.*[1]

When you're thirsty like this, no one has to tell you to drink when water comes along. Notice what happened to Exupéry when a Bedouin rescuer brought him water.

> *Face to the sand, we waited. And when the water came, we drank like calves with our faces in the basin, and with a greediness which alarmed the Bedouin so that from time to time he pulled us back. But as soon as his hand fell away from us we plunged our faces anew into the water.*[2]

People who are being readied by God for revival are first stricken with an unquenchable thirst for His glory. Blessed craving! But here's the good news (don't miss this!): *Your thirst is evidence that water exists to satisfy it!* Charles Spurgeon said, "When the Creator gives His creature the power of thirst, it is because water exists to meet its thirst; when He creates hunger there is food to correspond to the appetite; so when He inclines men to pray it is because prayer has a corresponding blessing connected with it."

People who are being readied by God for revival are first stricken with an unquenchable thirst for His glory.

In other words, prayer serves a purpose. We don't pray to engage in some symbolic act of piety that makes us feel holy. God has called us to prayer so He can give us a blessing! So obey your thirst! Claim God's promise to "pour water upon him that is thirsty, and floods upon the dry ground" (Isaiah 44:3, KJV). Know that your desire to pray is instigated by the God who waits to satisfy that desire.

Be specific

Don't be coy or vague with God. If you seek revival, be specific and ask for that very thing. With Hannah, there were no fuzzy generalities. Her problem was infertility ("The Lord had closed her womb" 1 Samuel 1:5). Her request was a son ("And she made a vow, saying, 'O Lord Almighty, if you will only look upon your servant's misery and remember me, and not forget your servant but give her a son, then I will give him to the Lord for all the days of his life . . .' " 1 Samuel 1:11).

Again, the disciples had been told to wait at Jerusalem for the promised gift of the Holy Spirit (see Acts 1:4, 5). There, "they all joined together constantly in prayer" (v. 14). "Now, in obedience to the word of the Saviour, the disciples offered their supplications for this gift, and in heaven Christ added His intercession. He claimed the gift of the Spirit, that He might pour it upon His people."[3]

They prayed for what was promised and received exactly what they asked for. Many prayer meetings fizzle because the pray-ers are unfocused, vague, and preoccupied with individual prayer requests. "Most prayer that takes place in church settings is not corporate prayer," writes *Pray!* Magazine editor Jonathan Graf. "It is more often individual prayer in a corporate setting."[4] Graf goes on to acknowledge that this kind of prayer, while important and valid, doesn't produce the kind of "one accord" mindset that was present at Pentecost. "True corporate prayer seeks God's face *as one body in one voice about one thing.*"[5]

When God's people pray corporately for revival, they are focused and specific about what they desire.

Fervency

Speaking of desire, fervency is another characteristic of prevailing prayer. Hannah's prayers for a child were anything but casual and haphazard. "In bitterness of soul Hannah wept much and prayed to the Lord" (1 Samuel 1:10). Eli the high priest accused her of being intoxicated when he observed her lips moving in silent prayer. But he had mistaken desire for drunkenness. (A common mistake made by those whose first love has grown cold!) " 'Not so, my lord,' " Hannah replied, " 'I am a woman who is deeply troubled. I have not been drinking wine or beer; I was pouring out my soul to the Lord. . . . I have been praying here out of my great anguish and grief' " (vs. 15, 16). Hannah's heart was set on having a child and she, like Jacob with the angel, was not going to let go until God blessed her! Do we desire the Holy Spirit like that?

Ellen White, writing about Jacob's night of wrestling with the angel, says this about fervency:

Jacob prevailed because he was persevering and determined. His victory is an evidence of the power of importunate prayer. All who will lay hold of God's promises, as he did, and be as earnest and persevering as he was, will succeed as he succeeded. Those who are unwilling to deny self, to agonize before God, to pray long and earnestly for His blessing, will not obtain it. Wrestling with God—how few know what it is! How few have ever had their souls drawn out after God with intensity of desire until every power in on the stretch.[6]

Again I'll ask it: do we desire the Holy Spirit like this? As was pointed out in an earlier chapter, most of us don't have time to eat breakfast, let alone time to wrestle with God for a blessing! If that scene in the thirty-second chapter of Genesis were played out today with us in the role of Jacob, a few minutes into the struggle our beepers would go off and we'd tell the angel, "Sorry, but I've got a call. I'll get back with you on that blessing thing."

With embarrassment I have to agree with Leonard Ravenhill who said, "A title, undeniably true of the Church today, would be *'We wrestle not!'* We pray with a 'take-it-or-leave-it' attitude; we pray chance prayers; we offer that which costs us nothing! We have not even 'strong desire.' We rather are fitful, moody and spasmodic."[7]

But those who are calling on God to bring back the glory of His favor will be fervent in their praying. Look closely at the prayer meeting in the Upper Room. Was there the slightest hint of casualness or nonchalance as they watched and waited for the promised Holy Spirit? Not on your life.

The disciples prayed with intense earnestness for a fitness to meet men and in their daily intercourse to speak words that would lead sinners to Christ. . . . The disciples felt their spiritual need and cried to the Lord for the holy unction that was to fit them for the work of soul saving.[8]

Is all of this talk of "wrestling" and "earnestness" making you nervous? I can hear some people as they read this shouting, "Legalism! More guilt! Works! Something else I'm not doing long enough or hard enough or sincere enough." My friend, I'm not trying to tell you what you MUST DO in order to experience revival. I'm simply stating the facts of what WILL BE in the life of the believer who "follows hard after God." Intensity is born of desire, and desire is born of need. The greater your need, the greater your desire. The greater your desire, the greater your intensity to pursue and obtain what you need. (See Luke 11:1-13; 18:1-8.)

Intensity is born of desire, and desire is born of need.

Many of you will remember the tragic climbing accident that occurred on Mt. Everest in 1996. *Into Thin Air* was the title given to both the book and film that chronicled the disaster. Among the survivors was Dr. Beck Weathers. His incredible story of survival and determination illustrates what need, desire, and intensity are all about:

> *On the night of May 10, 1996, a violent storm swept over Mt. Everest, buffeting the more than thirty adventurers who were descending from the mountain's summit with heavy snow, sub-zero cold, and hurricane-force winds. Within 24 hours, eight of the climbers, including three professional guides, were dead. It would become the deadliest day in the history of expeditions of the world's highest mountain.*
>
> *Among the climbers severely injured by the spring storm was Dr. Seaborn Beck Weathers, a forty-nine-year-old amateur climber who, lying unconscious and exposed on the mountain's icy rocks, had been*

left for dead three hundred yards from his camp. His wife and family were notified of his death.

Miraculously, Weathers awoke the morning after the storm to find himself alive, but barely. His hands were severely frostbitten; he had no feeling left in his feet; his vision was so impaired that he could see only three or four feet in front of him. But in his mind's eye, he could see his wife and children back home in Dallas, Texas. "I was lying on my back in the ice. It was colder than anything you can believe," he says. "I figured I had three or four hours left to live, so I started walking. All I knew was, as long as my legs would run, and I could stand up, I was going to move toward that camp, and if I fell down, I was going to get up. And if I fell down again, I was going to get up, and I was going to keep moving until I either hit that camp, I couldn't get up at all, or I walked off the face of that mountain."[9]

The need to survive fueled Beck Weathers' desire to make it off that mountain. No one had to tell him to be fervent in getting to safety. It wasn't legalism that moved Beck Weathers, it was his desire to live and see his wife and kids again. He was going to get to camp or die trying. *Oh that we would pray like this!* "Plead as earnestly, as eagerly, as you would for your mortal life, were it at stake," writes Ellen White. "Remain before God until unutterable longings are begotten within you for salvation, and the sweet evidence is obtained of pardoned sin."[10]

What could God accomplish through men and women who approached the throne of grace with this type of desire and intensity? Men and women who realize that without revival, without a burden for souls, they perish, and that they will pray towards this goal despite the "frostbite" that blackens their hearts? Though our spiritual vision be blurred by sin, dry eyes, and worldly affections, if, in our minds eye, we can see our own frozen condition as well as friends and loved ones who don't know the Lord and who are in peril as real as the peril

Dr. Weathers faced on Everest, we will begin to pray prevailing prayers! And if we fall, we'll get up. And if we fall down again, we'll get up again until the Lord blesses us!

United hearts

The Upper Room experience was a uniting experience. The 120 who had gathered there were "all with one accord in one place" (Acts. 2:1, KJV). They were "together, together" meaning in one place with one purpose. "All the disciples seem to have been present," Charles Finney notes. "They were all united and determined; their hearts were not alienated; there was union in prayer; all were united in one object. There was no person to remonstrate against their petition being granted; all were desirous to have this object accomplished."[11]

The Seventh-day Adventist Bible Commentary on Acts 2:1 says, "The ten days of expectancy had been ten days of earnest prayer (Acts 1:14), offered in unity of desire (AA 36, 37). This is the unity that must characterize the people of God whenever they aspire to a special experience with their Lord, or expect of Him a manifestation of power. Whatever interferes with such unity must be removed, or it will obstruct the Spirit, who does the work of God for His people."[12]

Christians are often their own worst enemy. It's a case of cannibalism—*sheep eating sheep!* I've often said that Satan doesn't need persecution to stop the church. Persecution is one of his "big guns" and he really doesn't want to use it because the church tends to grow under duress. But Satan doesn't have to rely on his big guns to topple us. Why use a cruise missile when a firecracker will do? Why use persecution when arguments over worship styles will split the church? Satan just doesn't have to work that hard to get us to break ranks with each other. Music, Bible translations, ethnicity, administrative positions, church offices or even favorite pews, are all the "firepower" he needs. The accuser sets off his little "firecrackers" and we go down like pins in a bowling alley! But when we finally figure out who our real enemy is and stop lobbing grenades of criticism and censure at each other, we will stand together as Jesus prayed we would (see John 17:20-23) and put the devil to flight with our united petitions against him. Prevailing prayer is united prayer.

Faith

The Bible says that faith is "the *substance* of things hoped for, the *evidence* of things not seen" (Hebrews 11:1, KJV, emphasis added). Notice that in this familiar definition of what faith is, there are two tangible elements ("substance" and "evidence") and two intangible elements ("things hoped for" and "things not seen") mentioned. Faith is not blind. It is not just super belief. Faith, genuine faith, has substance and evidence—tangible hooks on which we can hang our prayers.

If our prayers are to prevail with God, we must pray in faith, expecting a blessing. When Hannah finished praying in the temple, Eli told her, " 'Go in peace, and may the God of Israel grant you what you have asked of him' " (1 Samuel 1:17). Having thus obtained the "substance" of a word of assurance from the Lord, Hannah "went her way and ate something, and her face was no longer downcast" (v. 18). She stopped weeping and fasting and began waiting expectantly for the promised blessing. Later when she gave birth to a son, "she named him Samuel, saying, 'Because I asked the Lord for him' " (v. 20). Her unseen hope for a child rested on the "substance" of God's word through Eli. Her prayer of faith prevailed with God.

Likewise with the disciples, there was faith and expectation. Christ had told them that they would be baptized with the Holy Ghost and His promise was the substance of things they hoped for. "They knew that they had a Representative in heaven, an Advocate at the throne of God . . . . Higher and still higher they extended the hand of faith, with the mighty argument, 'It is Christ that died, yea rather, that is risen again, who is even at the right hand of God, who also maketh intercession for us' (Romans 8:34.)"[13]

Do we not have a Representative in heaven today? Do we have any "substance" or "evidence" for revival that we can hang our prayers on? Can we pray with the expectation of receiving what we pray for? Yes! Without a doubt. *Yes!* The evidence is the burden itself to pray. As we've already established, when God's people begin to thirst for revival, God is both the thirst-*maker* and the thirst *quencher*! Feeling dry? Rejoice! Showers of blessing are about to fall!

The "substance" of things unseen is God's promise that " 'If my people, who are called by my name, will humble themselves and pray and seek my face and turn from their wicked ways, then I will hear from heaven and will forgive their sin and heal their land' " (2 Chronicles 7:14).

But can we be sure this promise extends to our day? I see no statute of limitations on this text! As long as there are people called by God's Name who die to self and seek Him with all their hearts, and with repentance, this Word can be claimed. More than this, consider Jesus' last promise to His disciples, and to us.

> *He who promised that they should receive the Spirit not many days hence, said also "Go and disciple all nations, and Lo, I am with you always, even unto the end of the world." The meaning of this promise was everywhere you go, remember that I am with you; there lay hold on my strength, there believe on me, and I will manifest my presence. . . . You may always expect me, if you believe, to second your efforts; you may always expect the Holy Spirit to be poured out on you, and give effect to your honest efforts.*[14]

The race

Praying for revival is a marathon, not a sprint. God has called us to the race. Many of you have responded. You've begun. The start has been good. The prayer group you joined—great. The devotional habit you've started—super. The prayer partners you've acquired—wonderful. The "middle miles" though, are just up ahead.

"The middle miles are the tough ones. The cheering section is smaller here. You don't get as much encouragement from others. Routine sets in. You don't hear the voices shouting, 'Come on, you can make it'; 'Hang in there'; 'You're doing great.'

"Then your body starts to talk to you. 'Why are we doing this? Why don't we stop and rest awhile? We're going how far today?' You 'hit the wall,' as they call it, when your blood sugar drops and you feel as though you just can't put one foot in front of the other. That's hard.

"The starting line is behind you . . . the finish line seems so distant. It's the middle miles that are the hardest by far."[15]

I know this feeling well. Some mornings, prayer is more work than worship. More wrestling than relationship. I'm passionless, flat, uninspired. No burning bushes. No visions of Canaan. No still, small voices. Satan starts talking. "Why are you doing this? What real results are you seeing? Things around you aren't changing that much. Why don't you stop and rest awhile?" Know what I'm talking about? I "hit the wall."

What then? What will we do when we hit the wall and everything within us is wanting to quit? We don't quit. We P.U.S.H. (Pray Until Something Happens!)—until He sends His glory back into our lives.

Are you getting the picture that the kind of prayer we're talking about here is something out of the ordinary? Good. It is. Revival praying is not business as usual. It is as bold as Jacob wrestling with the Angel, as intense as an emergency room physician giving CPR and as determined as a half-frozen man crawling down a mountain and cheating death.

And still we've just scratched the surface. You know what? For most of my adult life I've been convinced that someday, somebody is going to take God at His Word and believe what He says. Somebody, somewhere is going to "Just Do It." "Someday," may as well be today. And "somebody" may as well be you and I. Together, let's press on and discover more principles for possessing Pentecost. Let's look into God's Word and find the fire that will consume our dross and ignite our passion for Christ.

In the next chapter we'll learn more of what happens when God's people pray for revival. Experiencing Pentecost may not be easy, but nothing worthwhile ever is. C'mon. *Let's do it!*

◆ ◆ ◆

A prayer

I've been AWOL lately, Lord. There's been too much noise, busyness,
sleepiness, indulgence, laziness—you name it. Bottom line:
I haven't wanted You enough to get here.
But I'm here now because I need You. I want You.
I desire to have Your divine power flow through me, Lord,
so that people are drawn to You. I want to want You as did the Psalmist
when he said he thirsts after You as the deer pants after the water.
My desire is weak, my conviction is slight.
I'm too easily satisfied with a surface knowledge and surface experience.
Increase my desire for Thee O Lord! Grow my hunger and capacity for You.
Amen.

---

1. As quoted in Douglas Cooper's, *Living God's Joy* (Mountain View, Calif.: Pacific Press Publishing Association, 1979), 14.
2. Ibid., 15.
3. Ellen White, *Acts of the Apostles,* p. 37.
4. Jonathan Graf, "One Voice, One Focus," *Pray!* Magazine, Jan/Feb 1999, p. 15.
5. Ibid. p. 15.
6. Ellen White, *The Great Controversy,* p. 621,emphasis added.
7. Leonard Ravenhill, *Why Revival Tarries* (Minneapolis: Bethany House Publishers, 1997 [1959]), 60.
8. *Acts of the Apostles*, 37, emphasis added.
9. http://speakers.com/bweathers.html
10. Ellen White, *Testimonies for the Church*, 1:63.
11. Charles G. Finney, "The Prevailing Prayer Meeting," sermon preached September 4, 1859 in Glasgow, Scotland (www.xmission.com/~gastown/revival/FINREV.TXT)
12. *Seventh-day Adventist Bible Commentary*, 6:135.
13. *Acts of the Apostles*, 35, 36.
14. Charles G. Finney, "The Prevailing Prayer Meeting," sermon preached September 4, 1859 in Glasgow, Scotland (www.xmission.com/~gastown/revival/FINREV.TXT)
15. Al McClure, "Middle Miles," *Adventist Review,* July 1996, p. 6.

" 'Do not leave Jerusalem, but wait for the gift my Father promised.' "

–Jesus (Acts. 1:4)

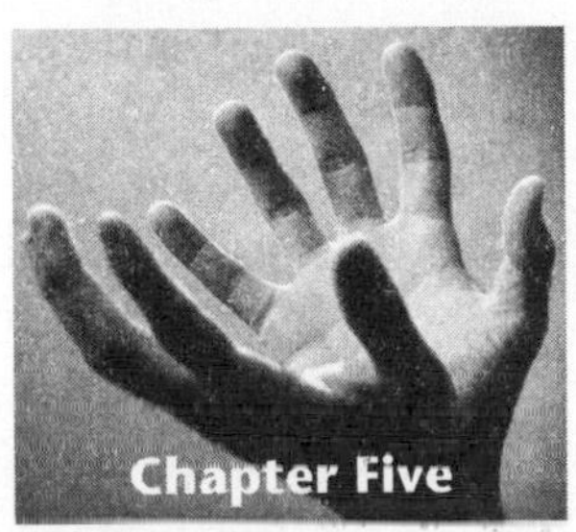

The GLORY of Waiting

A funny thing happened on the way to writing this chapter. I couldn't do it. I cramped up. My imagination server "crashed" and for a whole day my mental files locked up. I was frustrated and a little ticked off. I stared out the window. I paced the floor. I got in the car and drove to the post office to mail a package and to clear my head. When I got home, nothing had changed. The "system" was still down. Now what?

Feeling defeated, I went into the living room to pray. I was very tired and kept drifting off to sleep, so finally I stopped fighting it and napped for about 30 minutes. Later, I pulled a couple of my old prayer journals down from the shelf and began searching the pages. As I read, God began speaking to me through the words I had written to Him. One prayer in particular caught my eye. Someone else had written it, but I had copied it in my journal because it captured me so perfectly.

It would be easier for me to pray if I were clear and of a single mind and a pure heart;

if I could be done hiding from myself and from you, even in my prayers.
But I am who I am,
Mixture of motives and excuses,
Blur of memories, quiver of hopes,
Knot of fear, tangle of confusion,
and restless with love, for love.
I wander somewhere between gratitude and grievance,
wonder and routine, high resolve and undone dreams,
generous impulses and unpaid bills.
Come, find me, Lord. Be with me exactly as I am,
so I can begin to be yours.
Make of me something small enough to snuggle, young enough to question,
simple enough to giggle, old enough to forget,
foolish enough to act for peace;
skeptical enough to doubt the sufficiency of anything but you,
and attentive enough to listen as you call me out of the tomb of my timidity
into the chancy glory of my possibilities and the power of your presence.[1]

I thought of how accurately this prayer describes my inner struggle to become what God wants me to be. "Mixture of motives and excuses, knot of fear, tangle of confusion." Man, that's me! And as I meditated on this picture of who I am, realizing how many others reading this book also "wander somewhere between gratitude and grievance, wonder and routine, high resolve and undone dreams, . . ." God rebooted my "server." Once again I had access to my files, but they were slightly modified.

I want to spend a few moments talking about what happens after you pray for revival. After you say "Amen." So far we've talked about brokenness, the role of repentance and tears in revival. We've looked at "prevailing" prayer, desire, and how to pray the prayer of faith. But now, suppose you are ready to say Yes to the Lord?

Many of you will remember some definitive action you took the day you received Christ as your Savior or joined a church. There was probably an altar call of some kind. Maybe it was at church or at a camp meeting or under a canvass tent. The preacher extended an invitation and you "took your stand" for God and came down front for prayer, or signed a card, or raised your hand. You probably had Bible studies for a period of weeks or months, and then you were baptized in water as a symbol of your decision to follow Christ all the way. This is how many of us said Yes to God when we joined the church.

But what do you do when you've decided you want more? When you've heard God's call to prayer and repentance and you want to be filled with the Holy Spirit—to be used as an agent of revival? The answer that the Lord showed me is found in Jesus' words to the disciples just before He was taken from them back to heaven. " 'Do not leave Jerusalem, but **wait** for the gift my Father promised, which you have heard me speak about. For John baptized with water, but in a few days you will be baptized with the Holy Spirit' " (Acts 1:4, 5, emphasis added).

The glory of waiting

There it is. "Wait for the gift." Wait for the power. Not the answer you were looking for? I'm sorry. I don't like to wait either. But it's *how* we wait that makes all the difference. I wish to propose that the waiting we do is not passive, but active. Not sitting in a corner "looking intently up into the sky" as the disciples did watching Jesus disappear from sight, but actively waiting to receive our heart's desire. What are the steps?

First of all, *active waiting involves service.*

Look for opportunities to be a blessing to someone. Remember, the Holy Spirit comes not to make us super saints, but to empower us to serve.

Instead of living in expectation of some special season of excitement, we are wisely to improve present opportunities, doing that which must be done in order that souls may be saved. Instead of exhausting the powers of the mind in speculations in regard to the times and seasons which the Lord has placed in His own power, and withheld from men, we are to yield ourselves to the control of the Holy Spirit, to do present duties, to give the bread of life, unadulterated with human opinions, to souls who are perishing for the truth.[2]

Yesterday my daughter Crystal and I raked leaves for our neighbor next door. As I raked I prayed that God would use this simple act to provide an opportunity for me to share the gospel with my neighbor. I don't know when that opportunity will come, but I want to be ready and in position when it does come. God's word to Jeremiah and to us is, " 'Get yourself ready! Stand up and say to them whatever I command you' " (Jeremiah 1:17). Pray for opportunities to serve and to minister to others. As we wait on God for power to be His witnesses, let's put ourselves in a position to get wet when the showers of blessing begin to fall!

Fasting doesn't force God to do what we want. Fasting is a discipline that helps us humble ourselves so we can be more in tune with what God wants.

Fast and pray

I'll have more to say on spiritual fasting in the next chapter, but let's begin with some basics. Fasting doesn't force God to do what we want. Fasting is a discipline that helps us humble ourselves so we can be more in tune with what God wants. In the Sermon on the Mount, Jesus indicated that fasting would be part of the Christian experience. He said, "when you fast," not "*if* you fast." Rather than being an exercise in extreme piety, fasting is like a near-sighted person putting on glasses or a hearing-impaired person getting a hearing aid. It helps us hear God's voice with greater clarity.

There are many types of fasts, and it's important that you consult God as to what's the right fast for you. Will you fast for an entire day? One day a week? Will you miss only one meal? Will you limit your intake to water only or will you include juices? What about abstaining from TV, or the radio, or the Internet? What about giving your sweet tooth some time off and fasting from sweet desserts or meat? Whatever fast you choose, the important thing is to use the time you're not eating, or not watching TV to pray, to read God's Word and listen to His voice.

I personally like the idea of fasting one day a week. My hunger "pains" remind me that I have chosen to get closer to God that day and the growls are prompts to pray. I find this statement helpful: "When we fast, we have the opportunity to understand the meaning behind the words 'man does not live on bread alone, but on every word that comes from the mouth of the Lord' (Deuteronomy 8:3; Matt. 4:4). As we literally hunger and thirst after righteousness, we move from a concept to an experience. We discover that our souls indeed yearn for God like dry and thirsty lands where there is no water. We feel what it means for Jesus to be the Bread of Life."[3]

Active waiting on God means actively *listening* for His voice. Fasting clears the static of fast-paced, self-indulgent living on the phone lines of prayer so we can hear better.

United prayer

Notice this about the apostles as they waited in Jerusalem for the promised Holy Spirit. "They did not wait on the sovereignty of God without doing anything," observed Charles Finney, "but they waited in the agonizings of prayer with perpetual supplications."[4]

Also, Ellen White writing in *The Acts of the Apostles* said, "They did not wait in idleness. The record says that they were 'continually in the temple, praising and blessing God' (Luke 24:53). They also met together to present their requests to the Father in the name of Jesus."[5]

As the disciples "waited" in Jerusalem by being "continually in the temple, praising and blessing God," I want to propose a radical 3-point plan whereby we can do the same thing. None of these ideas is new or original with me. In fact, they are old strategies that are becoming new again as the spirit of prayer is once more animating the Church of Christ.

1. The Concert of Prayer. The Great Awakening (1725-1740) owes much to the movements of united prayer that preceded it. Count Nicholas Von Zinzendorf gathered a diverse group of Christians and set before them the goal of praying unitedly for God's blessing on the church. Called "Moravians," these Christians prayed 24 hours a day for more than 100 years. The flame they kindled through their prayers brought millions into the kingdom and ignited giants of revival such as John Wesley, George Whitefield, and Jonathan Edwards.

A new plan for united prayer emerged from the Great Awakening. Called "The Concert of Prayer," this plan, which lasted nearly 150 years, would become one of the most powerful schemes since the Reformation. This is how it worked: once a month or once a quarter, Christians from various churches would combine for joint prayer meetings, rotating the meeting from church to church, to pray for the outpouring of God's Spirit and the advancement of Christ's kingdom.[6]

I believe it's time for the concert of prayer to return to our church. That if we build houses of prayer, God will come in new glory! I recently conducted a prayer and revival conference in Gary, Indiana. Representatives from the four Adventist churches in Gary were present. One of the pastors there has a tremendous burden for the city of Gary coupled with an iron-clad belief in the power of prayer. When I left that city, I challenged the leaders to claim Gary for Jesus Christ and to establish the concert of prayer in their churches—to meet jointly for a "district-wide" prayer meeting once a month or once a quarter, specifically to pray for revival in the churches and in the city. Meeting jointly with other believers keeps the burden for revival fresh and energizes the members.

Another way to participate in the concert of prayer is from house to house. Establish "Houses of Prayer" (prayer groups) in the congregation, rotating the meetings from house to house. Once a quarter, let the prayer groups within the church come together for united prayer. This is a powerful way to "wait" on the Lord for the promised blessing and only God knows what the results will be.

2. The "closet" concert of prayer. Revivalist Charles Finney once encountered a group of women who had come to New York to observe the progress of revival there. They were impressed with the remarkable conversions that had occurred among some "hard cases" after special prayer was offered by church members. When asked if he thought it would be of any use for them to pray for a revival in their city, Finney encouraged them to go home and agree together with other women "to observe a closet concert of prayer for the outpouring of the Holy Spirit. They went home, and engaged some half dozen of them for that purpose, at sunrise, at midday, and at sunset. Three times a day they prayed for the outpouring of the Holy Spirit on their place."[7]

As a result of this "closet" concert of prayer, at the next church service, "no fewer than seventy individuals, who had been awakened, came together to be instructed by the deacons in regard to what they should do about the salvation of their souls, and a great revival followed."[8]

To begin a closet concert of prayer, simply agree with a partner or partners to pray for revival and souls at a specific time of day, and to do so faithfully no matter what else is going on. For months I participated with two other friends in a weekly closet concert of prayer. We agreed to pray from our homes or from wherever we happened to be at 4:30 a.m. every Tuesday morning. I still remember being in a hotel room in Atlanta, Georgia, and setting my alarm so I could unite with my brothers in their time zone for our weekly prayer time. We did not call each other on the phone for a conference-call prayer time. But there was power in knowing that at that moment, our voices were uniting as one in calling on the Lord for revival. What were the results of our closet concert? Well, I'm sure some of the fruit won't be seen until we reach the kingdom and see Jesus, but one result was a book entitled, *If My People Pray*[9] which has changed my life and the lives of many others. To God be the glory!

3. The daily prayer meeting. In the fall of 1999, the members of the Brooklyn Faith SDA Church participated in a 42-day prayer and fasting encounter that has left an indelible mark on that congregation*. Twice, during the 42 days I called the church—once to pray by phone with the members and once to speak with Sister Lurline Brown, prayer coordinator at Brooklyn Faith. I smiled as I heard the strains of "What A Friend We Have in Jesus" in the background as I spoke with Sister Brown. Here it was 10:00 or 11:00 in the morning on a weekday and the saints of God were gathered for prayer!

I had read about daily prayer meetings, but most churches I know wouldn't dare to attempt this type of thing today. In our times, when everyone is so "busy" and the mid-week prayer meeting is attended so poorly, the thought of opening the church for daily prayer boggles our minds. But here was a group of people actually doing it! They are among those I mentioned in the previous chapter who have gone beyond thinking about, wondering about, and hoping for revival.

I asked Sister Brown to write down her experiences and to share it with me in a letter. She graciously did so, and I'll share portions of that letter with you now.

> *The objective was to develop an awareness of the power of prayer and its potential to make a difference in everything we do. In addition, prayer should be seen as the life-line of the home, church, and its community. Subsequently, we need to tap into this source.*

With much prayer and help from the Holy Spirit, this plan was put into place. From September 30 to October 10, the session was held from 9:00 a.m. to 9:00 p.m. daily. On the first day the attendance was not encouraging, but by the evening session, the number of people grew to a surprising amount. As we progressed daily, the number gradually grew in attendance. On an average we had over 100 people going in and out as their schedules allowed. Time slots were set up in three-hour segments:

9 a.m. - 12 noon Praise & worship, Bible study, and prayer
12- 3 p.m. Lectures, praise and worship, and prayer
3 p.m. - 6 p.m. Lessons on prayer, and prayer workshops
6 p.m. - 8 p.m. Study The Great Controversy
8 p.m.- 9 p.m. Bible Study, doctrinal emphasis, and prayer

No one who entered this building left without prayer. Thus, the sick, burdened, and anyone who needed prayer came to be ministered to.

This encounter is the best thing that ever happened to this church. Individual lives have been changed; likewise families and the community at large. This encounter allowed people from all walks of life, denominations, and religious persuasions to come together for prayer. To be specific, there were Catholics, Jehovah Witnesses, Pentecostals, Rastafarians, and Methodists in attendance. One Methodist sister after two weeks attendance publicly stood up and declared her desire to be baptized, and she was. Police officers who patrolled the neighborhood became friendly with the church family as they, too, after being invited, would come by freely for prayer.

Several prayer walks and tract distributions were done in the neighborhood and prayer warriors prayed with people on the street also. On Thursdays, a flow of over 200 people were ministered to through the Community Service Department Food Distribution

Program. As a result of this program, there are now several candidates for Bible studies and follow up.

Other featured activities during this exercise encompassed health lectures, cooking classes, and lifestyle enrichment seminars. The grand finale was an all-night prayer vigil, baptism, and anointing services. Nineteen souls were baptized including a few re-baptisms. Pastor Noble Alexander, a visiting pastor and author of the book I Will Die Free[10] *did the honors at this closing exercise. It was a solemn, yet awesome encounter, and as of today no one who entered the church will be the same, because they have experienced the Man of Galilee.*

Praise the Lord! There is hunger for God in New York City! Is there hunger for God in your city, in your church, today? How about it? Could God be calling you to actively wait on Him in a citywide concert of prayer, a closet concert of prayer, or a daily prayer meeting?

I know that some of these suggestions seem "out there" on the fringe of reality. But my friends, isn't it time to dispense with business as usual and get serious with God? We need to start expecting God to impact us beyond the confines of the church bulletin! How long are we going to strait-jacket the Holy Spirit with our cherished "order of service?" What if God wants the pastor to give the appeal at the beginning of the sermon rather than at the end? Could we handle it?

We need to start expecting God to impact us beyond the confines of the church bulletin!

I'll never forget what happened to me during a Friday night prayer service in central London. After 45 minutes of praying with strangers who were brought in off the streets surrounding the church, the church was buzzing with excitement. The prayer conference was to resume with me delivering the message. But as I looked over that expectant audience, a dozen of whom were "street people" who, remarkably, had agreed to stay and worship with us after receiving prayer, I couldn't go forward with business as usual. For the second time that evening, the Holy Spirit preempted the program. As I took the platform to speak, I was impressed that God wanted an appeal made for salvation right then—*before* the sermon. I turned to pastor Hamilton Williams and told him what I felt God was wanting us to do. I sort of put the pastor on the spot, but he was willing to let the Lord take control of the program, and he gave the appeal. While the congregation sang, six or seven of our visiting friends—people who before that night had never set foot in that church—came to the altar to receive Jesus Christ as the Lord of their lives! Hallelujah!

Some came sobbing, as did a young man with long blond hair, smelling of alcohol, sitting with head buried in his lap as he sat on the altar steps, crying out for God to come into his life. God granted me the privilege and honor of praying with this young man and his brother. In their brokenness I was given a glimpse of God's glory, and as I led these young men to Jesus, I realized that I was standing, with them and everyone else in that building, on holy ground.

If I never see another bulletin again I won't cry. But if we don't begin to see more of God's glory in our services, let us fill an ocean with our tears!

But what if we hadn't been willing to surrender the pulpit to Jesus? What if we had followed the "program" and gone ahead with business as usual? If we're so tied to the bulletin that the Holy Spirit can't move, *get rid of the bulletin!* Jesus is about to come! Just maybe, the times call for something beyond "Opening Song, Scripture, Opening Prayer, Special Music, and the Sermon." God help us! It's not about a program, it's about seeking His face for a return of His glory! It's about surrendering control and convention and getting on our faces and crying out to God to send rain or we perish! If I never see another bulletin again I won't cry. But if we don't begin to see more of God's glory in our services, let us fill an ocean with our tears!

Lastly, *to wait means to persevere.*

We looked at this a little in the previous chapter, but I want to dig a little deeper. I have often been asked why it is necessary to keep asking God for something. Doesn't this amount to a lack of faith? Why not just ask once and leave it with God to answer according to His wisdom and timing? These are reasonable questions. And I think sometimes, it is appropriate to take this approach. However, it is interesting to note that on two separate occasions when Jesus was teaching on prayer, He used two stories that both featured characters who persisted in their asking until they got what they wanted (see Luke 11:5-10; 18:1-8).

Different situations call for different actions in prayer. On Mount Carmel, Elijah prayed once for God to show Himself to be the true God, and fire fell instantly from heaven. But when he prayed for rain to return to the land, Elijah "bent down to the ground and put his face between his knees" seven times before clouds began to gather (see 1 Kings 18:42-45). Even the Son of God petitioned His Father three times to let the cup of Calvary pass.

The list of reasons why perseverance in prayer is necessary is long. But let's explore at least three of these.

1. Satanic resistance. In Daniel 10, we read about a vision that was given to Daniel concerning a great war. Daniel fasted and prayed for three weeks waiting for the understanding of what he'd seen. While standing on the bank of the Tigris River, Daniel suddenly saw "a man dressed in linen, with a belt of the finest gold around his waist. His body was like chrysolite, his face like lightning, his eyes like flaming torches, his arms and legs like the gleam of burnished bronze, and his voice like the sound of a multitude" (Daniel 10:5, 6).

The other men with Daniel did not see what he saw but were suddenly overcome with a sense of terror, causing them to run for cover. Daniel fell to the ground, powerless until the angel touched him and gave him strength.

" 'Do not be afraid, Daniel,' " the angel said. " 'Since *the first day* that you set your mind to gain understanding and to humble yourself before your God, your words were heard, and I have come in response to them. But the prince of the Persian kingdom *resisted me twenty-one days*' " (vv. 12, 13, emphasis added).

Daniel was unaware of the war in the heavens while he prayed! The "prince of the Persian kingdom" or Satan, was determined that light from heaven did not get through to Daniel, and he's still just as determined today. "At every revival of God's work the prince of evil is aroused to more intense activity; he is now putting forth his utmost efforts for a final struggle against Christ and His followers."[11]

We need to remember that "our struggle is not against flesh and blood, but against the rulers, against the authorities, against the powers of this dark world and against the spiritual forces of evil in the heavenly realms" (Ephesians 6:12). The enemy will do everything in his power to keep us from the one thing that will utterly defeat him—prayer. Therefore, we need to persevere.

2. Unreadiness to receive. When my oldest daughter Candice was 11 years old, she wanted to drive. Being tall for her age, she was physically capable of steering the car and reaching the pedals. What if I had given her the keys and with a smile and a wave said, "Have a good time, Sweetheart. See you when you get home." I would have been arrested for felony child endangerment and held liable for all the injuries caused in the wrecks she surely would have had! To give my daughter the keys at 11 when she had no training, no practice behind the wheel of "a three-ton death machine" as we like to call it, would be completely irresponsible. Nothing wrong with the desire to drive, but the timing just wasn't right.

Five years later, when she had gone to driving school, spent the required hours behind the wheel, and passed her written Idaho State driver's exam, Candice received her driver's license and I was happy (not really) to hand her the keys to the car. The request and the desire were exactly the same. The difference now was that she was ready to receive the blessing.

Sometimes we're not ready to receive the thing we're asking for. In His mercy, God delays the answer to our prayers until we are ready. While we wait for the blessing, we're to persevere and not give up.

3. To intensify desire. Children are impulsive. Take them to the store and they'll ask for everything in sight. Experienced parents know that most of these requests will disappear from memory once you leave the store. Out of sight, out of mind. But every now and then the kids will latch onto something and won't let go. Such was the case when my girls wanted a dog. With apologies to Luke 18, I'll relate my story of "The Persistent Daughter."

In a certain town there was a mom and dad who feared God but could care less about dogs. And there was a daughter in the home of this mom and dad who kept coming to them with the plea, "grant me a puppy, please!"

For some time they refused. The struggle intensified. The begging, bargaining, promising, and pleading continued day and night. But the mom and dad held firm.

Once, before persistent daughters came into their lives, there were always two aisles in the supermarket the mom and dad could breeze by—the baby aisle and the pet supplies aisle. Their favorite cry as they quickly scooted past these aisles was "No dogs and no babies!"

The cry in recent years had gotten considerably weaker, what with the "No babies" part dropping off into obsolescence. But they weren't going to surrender the "No dogs" part without a fight.

Prayers were prayed, pictures were drawn. My daughter even wrote a book on the computer called, *My Dog*. Once, a puppy—one of six siblings being given away for free outside of Shopko—almost made it from the dad's arms to the car. Until the chilling stare of the mom quickly banished such foolish thoughts from the dad's temporarily fogged head.

Finally the dad said to himself, "Even though I fear God and could care less about dogs, yet because this daughter keeps bothering me, I will see that she gets a puppy, so that she won't eventually drive me to drink with her begging!"

And that's exactly what happened. A week before I got Chloe, I told the girls that if they didn't bother me, I would have a decision by the following WEDNESDAY. On FRIDAY I went to the animal shelter and found a 5-month-old black and white terrier mutt. Adoption day was TUESDAY—one day *before* the decision deadline.

All weekend they were killing themselves trying not to talk about the dog, but they did keep me aware that Wednesday was coming. They were hopeful, anxious. *But I already knew what I was going to do!* They didn't know it but the answer to their prayer had already been granted. *They just hadn't come into possession of it yet!*

Tuesday evening—a day before the deadline—I picked up the puppy. As I pictured their reaction, my pulse began to race. I couldn't get home fast enough. I couldn't wait to see their faces! When I walked into the house with Chloe in my arms, there was instant bedlam. Joy unrestrained. Shouts of "I can't believe it!" "Thank you! Thank you!" and spontaneous dance broke out in our household. It was quite a spectacle. And, here's the point I want you to get, Suzette and I took as much or more pleasure in watching their joy as they took in receiving their long-awaited puppy.

The point: Before you call, God has answered. Your today and your tomorrow is already in God's past. He's seen it all and knows what He's going to do. We've all experienced delays. Times when it appeared God didn't answer, or at least didn't hear. We've all begged, bargained, and pleaded for things seemingly to no avail. And yet, our most basic prayer and plea—"Lord, save me!" has been answered. Isn't it a comfort to you to know that in answer to your plea for salvation, Jesus' answer is "In my Father's house are many mansions: if it were not so, I would have told you. I go to prepare a place for you. And if I go and prepare a place for you, I will come again, and receive you unto myself; that where I am, there ye may be also" (John 14:2, 3, KJV).

Your today and your tomorrow is already in God's past. He's seen it all and knows what He's going to do.

We wait, as did my daughter for her puppy, anxiously, hoping against all hope that we will be saved. Prayers have been prayed, pictures have been painted, stories told, books written, sermons preached about the day Jesus will come to save us and put an end to sin and the suffering it's caused. Jesus, who doesn't need to be begged to answer this prayer, is already at work preparing the house that you will occupy in glory. His pulse is beginning to race in anticipation of your homecoming.

As we continue to pray, and toil, and suffer, and wait, He is already picturing that reunion day when He'll come for us in the clouds, and the excitement is beginning to get to Him. On that day, there will be bedlam. Joy unrestrained. Shouts of "I can't believe it!" "Thank You! Thank You!" and spontaneous dance will break out across the planet. It will be quite a spectacle.

As He chooses your favorite colors and textures for your custom-built mansion, He already sees the expression on your face, hears the praises from your lips, and feels the vibrations beneath His feet as you leap for joy and fall to your knees in unspeakable gratitude. And again, the Father will take as much or more pleasure in watching our joy than we will have in receiving our long-awaited Savior.

Keep believing. Keep praying. Keep waiting. Before you call, God has answered. Your today and your tomorrow is already in God's past. He's seen it all and knows exactly what He's going to do.

A prayer

"And now, Lord, what wait I for? my hope is in thee" (Psalm 39:7, KJV).
I am so tired of doing the church "thing" and not seeing Your glory.
Help me to actively wait on You for power to do Your will.
And if it means an end to business as usual, so be it.
Time is short and I long to be with You.
I'm so glad to know that You are longing to be with me.
Give me, I pray, a single mind and a pure heart.
Call me from the tomb of my timidity and show me the glory of who I can become in You.
Amen.

---

1. Ted Loder, *Guerrillas of Grace* (San Diego, Calif.: Lura Media, 1984).
2. Ellen G. White, *Evangelism*, p. 702.
3. Cindy Hyle Bezek, "Has the Fast-food Generation Missed Out?" *Pray!* Magazine, Nov/Dec, 1997, p. 17, 18.
4. From "The Prevailing Prayer Meeting," by Charles G. Finney, Preached September 4, 1859, Glasgow, Scotland. (www.xmission.con/~gastown/revival/FINREV.TXT)
5. Ellen G. White, *The Acts of the Apostles*, p. 35.
6. Robert Bakke, "Prayer: God's Catalyst for Revival," *Pray!* Magazine, issue one, 1997, p. 16, 17.
7. From "The Prevailing Prayer Meeting," by Charles G. Finney, Preached September 4, 1859, Glasgow, Scotland. (www.xmission.con/~gastown/revival/FINREV.TXT)
8. Ibid.
9. (Nampa, Idaho: Pacific Press Publishing Association, 1995).

* In October, 1998, after praying for God's direction in putting together the prayer ministry plans for 1999, Lurline Brown felt impressed by the Holy Spirit to have a 40-day prayer encounter. At the Northeastern Conference Prayer Warriors monthly meeting and workshop in January, 1999, Sister Brown presented her plan. It was there she discovered that Conference Coordinator Patricia Langley had a similar plan, the difference being two additional days to accommodate an in-depth study of the book, *The Great Controversy.* After consultation with the Brooklyn Faith pastor, the two women merged their plans and the 42-day encounter was born.

10. (Nampa, Idaho: Pacific Press Publishing Association, 1991).
11. Ellen G. White, *The Great Controversy*, p.593.

As soon as we cease to bleed, we cease to bless.
–Dr. J. H. Jowett

When believers lacking births become burdened,
and when soul-sterility sickens us, then we will pulsate with holy fear,
and pray with holy fervor, and produce with holy fertility.
–Leonard Ravenhill

" 'If you can do anything, take pity on us and help us.' "
–Mark 9:22

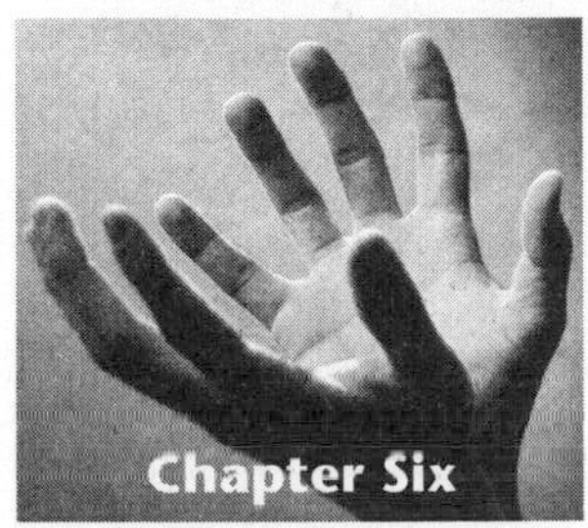

The GLORY of Compassion

The question startled me. It blind-sided me and left me praying to God for help. The setting was a canvass tent at the South Lake Tahoe camp meeting. I was presenting a workshop on how to transform churches into houses of prayer. It was my second session of the day and the afternoon heat was making everyone a little drowsy and sticky. I was already into my presentation when a gentleman leaned forward on his chair and shot me a question that forced me to look away from my overhead transparencies.

"I want to know something," he started. I innocently asked him to continue, though I had a premonition that this question was intended to test me as much as it was to get an answer. He proceeded. "We organized prayer groups for Net '96, and still only baptized one person. What I want to know is what happened? We prayed and it didn't work. Why?"

Well, I don't mind telling you that for a moment I froze as if I had seen a bear and was playing dead. I had no idea how to answer this gentleman and I certainly didn't want to make something up that sounded trite and predictable. In that instant, I had a "Nehemiah moment"

(Nehemiah 2:4) and shot a quick prayer to God for help. Just as quickly the Lord impressed me to ask the gentleman a question.

"I can't say for sure why the results weren't greater," I began, "but let me ask you a question."

"Sure," he responded.

"Before Net '96 began, did your church pray for the community?" He sat silent. "And now that Net '96 is over, and you have your one soul, are you still praying for the community? For the ones who didn't come?" The gentleman's eyes fell and he slowly shook his head, acknowledging that when the crusade ended, so did the prayer effort.

With all my heart I believe that one of the reasons God can't bless our evangelism with greater results is because our love for the lost is programmed. We "love" them when the calendar tells us it's time to do evangelism, but "drop" them the second the credits begin to roll on the final satellite telecast. God, forgive us!

During the summer of 1998 a friend of mine called and mentioned his disappointment at the poor results his Net '98 flyers were getting in his neighborhood. He was taking the flyers door-to-door but there seemed to be very little interest.

"How well do you know your neighbors?" I asked. "Not very," he replied.

"Have you had much contact with them before now?"

"No," he admitted.

"Well, put yourself in their shoes," I said. "If someone you barely knew stuck a piece of paper in your hand inviting you to meetings at a church you were unfamiliar with, to hear a speaker you've never heard of, would *you* go?"

He laughed and said "Not a chance."

"Well, what makes you think your neighbors are going to react any differently?"

My friend got the point, but I wonder if we do. Jesus commanded us to go and make *disciples*, but most of us don't even know how to make *friends*! The sad thing about our evangelism efforts is not the small results, but the lack of caring about those small results. We'll finish an 8-week satellite series, have one or no baptisms to show for it, wipe our hands and calmly go on to Ingathering, Pathfinder Sabbath, women's retreat, or whatever else is next up on the church calendar without even pausing to debrief and question our lack of soul-winning effectiveness. Why is that? Simply put, *we don't really care*. If seeing those words in print stung, believe me, I felt the pain as I typed them. And I won't hide behind the "we" in that sentence. *I* don't care. Not really. Not the way Jesus wants me to care. I have to be honest. I'm not losing sleep over the spiritual condition of my neighbors. I'm not upset about the people who live around my church who don't know the truth. But praise God, it's beginning to bother me!

Jesus commanded us to go and make disciples, but most of us don't even know how to make friends!

One of the marks of genuine revival is a rekindled love for the lost. A return of compassion. An alignment (finally!) of our agenda with God's! Think about it. If God did sleep, what would keep Him up at night? Wouldn't it be the salvation of His children? Well, we know that God never sleeps or slumbers (see Psalm 121:4). He's "up" all day and all night with only one item on His "To Do" list: redemption.

When a mysterious explosion rocked the Apollo 13 command module on April 13, 1970, the now famous cry from space, "Houston, we have a problem," gripped a nation with fear and a sense of terrible urgency. Frantic flight directors, mission specialists, and astronauts at Mission Control crowded around workstations designed for one, and worked around the clock, ignoring shift changes, determined to bring the crippled ship and its crew home. Vacation plans were scrubbed, dinner plans interrupted, "normal" life was put on hold. A life and death drama was playing itself out in deep space and in Houston the salvation of Astronauts Lovell, Swigert, and Haise was the only focus, the only goal, the only agenda.

When a mysterious explosion called sin rocked spaceship earth, the cry of earth's inhabitants caught the ear of Almighty God. Heaven's "Mission Control" went into full action and every spiritual agency was set into operation to bring the lost sons of God home. "Normal" life in heaven was put on hold. A life and death drama of the ages was playing itself out on planet Earth, and in heaven, the salvation of humankind was and is the only focus, the only goal, the only agenda.

"Oh, think" writes Ellen White, "of the yearning desire Christ has to bring to His fold again those who have gone astray!"[1] Ask yourself: if God is our Father and Jesus our Brother, how can we care so little about the things they care so much about? Why do we pray so little for what weighs heaviest on the heart of God?

I've seen "Christians" nearly come to blows over drama, drums, or carpeting, and yet remain silent when the baptistry remains dry from lack of use. I've seen saints angry enough to leave church when their favorite seat was taken by a visitor, but never offer a word of protest when the church goes on year after year without witnessing a soul coming to Christ! "The trouble with many believers," writes Leonard Ravenhill, "is that they are angry over trifles and are unmoved about tragedies. They are angry because of some personal slight, but are sphinx-like while the wolves of lust devour our youth and while demons of false doctrine scatter the flock."[2] My friends, we've got it backwards. We're living life, as the Truth song says, "upside down."

The church is to be a source of healing and comfort in the community, but sadly, the community barely knows we exist.

A source of healing and comfort?

The church is to be a source of healing and comfort in the community, but sadly, the community barely knows we exist. Imagine that space aliens zapped your current place of worship and tomorrow morning your church was gone—sucked right off its foundation. Nothing left but a gaping hole where your church used to sit. How many days would go by before someone in the neighborhood noticed the church was missing? If you can say that the neighbors would notice immediately, then praise the Lord! You are letting your light shine and making an impact on those around you. But if yours is like many other churches, the answer might be days, weeks, or even *years!*

The truth of this was brought home to me in a painful way not long ago when I conducted a prayer "experiment" in the neighborhood surrounding my own local church. It was Wednesday night, and I was leading out in prayer meeting. I asked for a few volunteers to go knock on doors in the apartment complex less than a hundred yards from our church building. They were to go in twos and introduce themselves to people as their neighbors from the Seventh-day Adventist Church and offer to pray with them. Those remaining in the church were instructed to pray for the volunteers—that God would bless them as they made contact with the community. After only 15 minutes, the volunteers returned with more than a dozen prayer requests! That was the *good* news.

The bad news was that one of the people contacted—a young man—didn't realize there was a church on his street! My parents were the ones who knocked on this young man's door. They pointed down the street and said, "Sure, we're from the church right over there." When the young man still shrugged in perplexity, my mom literally took him by the hand to the railing on his second-floor apartment landing and pointed to the building a stone's throw away saying, "See?"

"Ohhhh," said the young man. "I wondered what cars were doing at that building on Saturdays. I didn't know it was a church."

Imagine! A person living almost within the shadow of our church, not even knowing we existed. That was the extent of the impact we had made on his life up until that evening, and sadly, that is the way it is for many of us. Leonard Ravenhill said it best:

> *At the very doors of our churches are the masses—unwon because they are unreached, unreached because they are unloved. Thank God for all that is being done for missions overseas. Yet it is strangely true that we can get more "apparent" concern for people across the world than for our perishing neighbors across the street!*[3]

How can we claim to be "ready" for Jesus to come, when so many of those around us—including friends and loved ones—aren't ready to meet Him? Why doesn't this bother us more than it does? Do we really believe Jesus is coming? Do we really believe there's a heaven and a second death? Do we believe that without a saving knowledge of Christ, many will perish needlessly? Do we care?

The story is told about a criminal named Charlie Peace who was condemned to death in an English prison. On the morning of his execution he was taken to the death chamber accompanied by the prison chaplain who was sleepily reading some Bible verses. Charlie asked the preacher what he was reading. "The Consolations of Religion" was the reply. Charlie was shocked at the matter-of-fact manner in which the preacher was reading about hell. Could a man be so unmoved under the very shadow of the scaffold as to lead a fellow-human there and yet, dry-eyed, read of eternal separation of the sinner from God? How could he slide over the passages he was reading without so much as a tremor in his voice?

"Sir," Charlie addressed the chaplain, "if I believed what you and the church of God *say* you believe, even if England were covered with broken glass from coast to coast, I would walk over it, if need be, on hands and knees and think it worthwhile living, just to save one soul!"

O God! Forgive me for my selfishness! Break this hard heart and tenderize it to care for those who don't know you!

Getting Started

Where do we begin? How do we develop genuine concern and love for the lost?

1. Pray to love Jesus more.

Vance Havner wrote: "The primary qualification for a missionary is not love for souls, . . . but love for Christ." We need to "see" Jesus again. Embrace His mission, observe His passion. And what is His passion? Remember and meditate with me:

> *"As Jesus stepped into the garden, you were in His prayers. As Jesus looked into heaven, you were in his vision. As Jesus dreamed of the day when we will be where he is, he saw you there. His final prayer was about you. His final pain was for you. His final passion was you."*
>
> *He wanted out, but he couldn't because he saw you. "He saw you cast into a river of life you didn't request. He saw you betrayed by those you love. He saw you with a body which gets sick and a heart which grows weak. . . . He saw you in your Garden of Gethsemane—and he didn't want you to be alone. . . . The final battle was won in Gethsemane. And the sign of conquest is Jesus at peace in the olive trees. For it was in the garden that he made his decision. He would rather go to hell for you than go to heaven without you."* [4]

It is this Jesus that we need to fall in love with again. As we do so, He will give us His heart of love for your brothers and sisters that He saw along with you that night in the garden.

2. Adopt the Lord's Fast.

Fasting is often promoted as the secret weapon in revival praying. As noted in the previous chapter, the practice of fasting is essentially a denial of self in order to seek God. When we think of fasting, we primarily think of abstaining from food, but the prophet Isaiah introduces us to another fast that pleases the Lord even more.

> *"Is not this the kind of fasting I have chosen: to loose the chains of injustice and untie the cords of the yoke, to set the oppressed free and break every yoke? Is it not to share your food with the hungry and to provide the poor wanderer with shelter–when you see the naked, to clothe him, and not turn away from your own flesh and blood?" (Isaiah 58:6, 7).*

This is the Lord's fast. It is a fast from selfishness. A fast from thinking about your own ease and comfort. When you fast from self, you focus on God, and when you focus on God, you see what He sees and hear what He hears. And what does God see? His children suffering. What does God hear? The cries of His children who are hungry, alone, poor, trapped, abused, tormented, addicted, etc.

But when we're adopting the Lord's fast we do more than see and hear, we ACT. We don't just sit in our homes and wait for our next meal. We "loose the chains of injustice and untie the cords of the yoke, to set the oppressed free and break every yoke." We "share [our] food with the hungry and provide the poor wanderer with shelter . . ." In other words, WE GET INVOLVED! And what will be the result when we do?

> *"Then your light will break forth like the dawn, and your healing will quickly appear; then your righteousness will go before you, and the glory of the Lord will be your rear guard. Then you will call, and the Lord will answer; you will cry for help, and he will say: Here am I. . . The Lord will guide you always; he will satisfy your needs in a sun-scorched land and will strengthen your frame. You will be like a well-watered garden, like a spring whose waters never fail" (vs. 8, 9, 11).*

The GLORY of Compassion

Revival! For every one of us who thirsts for the refreshing water of a Holy Spirit outpouring, here is the fountainhead! God has not hidden the keys to revival from us, we just insist on using our own set. We must stop this adolescent inward focus on *our* wants, *our* needs, *our* thirst, and begin to pray to be like Jesus who said, " 'the Son of Man did not come to be served, but to serve, and to give his life as a ransom for many' " (Matthew 20:28).

Notice what can happen when we get on the same wavelength with God: "As the will of man co-operates with the will of God," writes Ellen White, "it becomes omnipotent."[5] All powerful! But when the will of man pushes the agenda of *man*, it becomes impotent.

Think about it. For three and a half years the disciples' main concern was themselves—their status in Christ's new kingdom; their ranking in the apostolic pecking order. Even while Jesus was preparing to make the ultimate sacrifice for them, they were consumed with who among them was the greatest.

But later, after Jesus' ascension into heaven, they gathered in the upper room to wait for the promised Holy Spirit. And when they prayed for a burden for souls, "there came a sound. . . as of a rushing mighty wind,. . . tongues like as of fire, . . . sat upon each of them. . . they were all filled with the Holy Ghost, and began to speak with other tongues, as the Spirit gave them utterance " (Acts 2:2-4, KJV).

When all we're interested in is "good church," when we settle for "respectable" Christianity where we become professional church-goers, when we get pushed out of shape because sister so-and-so got elected to be Sabbath School Superintendent again, or because so-and-so is always asked to sing solos in the choir, or because we never get to plan the church potluck, we echo the selfish struggle of the disciples before Pentecost. We're impotent. We have no power to change our own spiritual diapers let alone power to change a morally bankrupt culture that's perishing in darkness. But when we put forth prayer and energy, and focus on the priorities of God—the saving of souls—we can tell a world crippled in sin and degeneracy "In the name of Jesus Christ, arise and walk!" And they will!

When we put forth prayer and energy, and focus on the priorities of God . . . we can tell a world crippled in sin and degeneracy "In the name of Jesus Christ, arise and walk!" And they will!

---

3. Start befriending your neighbors.

You can't love someone if you never talk to them. And don't start with a Bible study on the Sabbath! I have a dear friend who just moved in next door to an elderly Adventist couple. My friend happens not to be of our faith, but he is a warm, dedicated Christian gentleman. He loves the Lord Jesus with all his heart and I consider it a privilege to be his friend. I wish I could say that my friend's encounter with his new neighbor was as positive.

On only their second meeting, the Adventist neighbor saw my friend and his wife returning home from Easter Sunday services at church and, after a few pleasantries, proceeded to question my friend's Christianity because of his day of worship! Now some might call that evangelism. I just call it *rude!*

This well-meaning gentleman hadn't earned the right to intrude into something so personal as one's religious convictions. Be a friend first. Show what Mrs. White calls, "disinterested love" to your neighbor. Look for ways to help and bless them, and then pray for opportunities to share with them what Jesus has done for you.

"If we would humble ouselves before God, and be kind and courteous and tenderhearted and pitiful, there would be one hundred conversions to the truth where now there is only one."[6]

4. Prayer-walk your neighborhood.

To begin transforming your church into a source of healing and comfort for the community, try prayer-walking the neighborhood. Prayer-walking is the practice of walking the streets of your community while praying, or "praying on-site with insight." Prayer-walkers should go in teams of two—preferably male/female or female/female, but never male/male. When the person answers the door, introduce yourselves as neighbors from the church and tell them you're in the community to offer prayer on behalf of the residents.

You get some really interesting reactions! First is reluctant shock, then there's a softening at the warm gesture being extended to them. If they are willing, pray with them on the spot. Otherwise, note their request, wish them God's blessings, and leave.

I've developed a simple "calling card" that can be left at any home prayer-walkers call on.

It has "Someone Cares" in large type across the top followed by a line indicating the day and time that home was prayed for. The church's address, phone, and worship services follow. The card can be left with the person who answers the door, or left in the doorjamb or screen when no one is home. I created this card on my computer using the business card template on WordPerfect 8. They're printed on Avery 5371 Laser white business cards that you can purchase at any office supply store.

Wouldn't it be wonderful if instead of knowing you by your diet or by your day of worship, members of the community knew you as "the people who come and pray for me"?

5. Establish evangelism prayer teams.

Get small teams of people to pray for visitors during the church service. Pray for the pastor as he preaches and pray that his message hits a responsive chord in the visitors' hearts as they listen. Rotate the teams from week to week and encourage the pastor to make some form of appeal at the end of every sermon. This will help the entire congregation start thinking evangelistically, and as decisions are made for Christ, the members will be energized with the rediscovery of the gospel's power to change lives.

We sing the hymn "Does Jesus Care?"[7] and answer triumphantly on the refrain, "O yes, He cares—I know He cares!" Well, if Jesus lives in us, we will care too. The Revival Generation will be a Compassionate Generation–a people who love Jesus enough to love the people He died for. This is our calling, our heritage and our ticket to revival.

◆ ◆ ◆

A prayer

Oh! for a heart that is burdened!
Infused with a passion to pray;
Oh! for a stirring within me;
Oh! for His power every day.
Oh! for a heart like my Saviour,
Who, being in an agony, prayed.
Such caring for OTHERS, Lord, give me;
On my heart let burdens be laid.
My Father, I long for this passion,
To pour myself out for the lost–
To lay down my life to save others–
"To pray," whatever the cost.
Lord, teach me, Oh teach me this secret,
I'm hungry this lesson to learn,
This passionate passion for others,

For this, blessed Jesus, I yearn.
Father, this lesson I long for from Thee–
Oh, let Thy Spirit reveal this to me.
–Mary Warburton Booth

---

[1] Ellen G. White, *Christian Service*, p.169

[2] Leonard Ravenhill, *Revival Praying* (Minneapolis: Bethany House Publishers, 1996 [1962]), 131.

[3] Leonard Ravenhill, *Why Revival Tarries* (Minneapolis: Bethany House Publishers, 1997 [1959]), 110.

[4] Max Lucado, *And the Angels Were Silent*, pp. 154, 155.

[5] Ellen G. White, *Christ's Object Lessons*, p. 333.

[6] Ellen G. White, *Testimonies* 9:189

[7] Frank E. Graeff and J. Lincoln Hall, "Does Jesus Care?", *The Seventh-day Adventist Hymnal* (Hagerstown, Md.: Review and Herald Publishing Association, 1985), #181.

If there were a drunken orgy somewhere,
I would bet ten to one a church member was not in it.
But if there were a lynching,
I would bet ten to one a church member was in it.
–Robert Miller in *American Protestantism and Social Issues*

"How long, O Lord?"
–Rev. 6:10, KJV

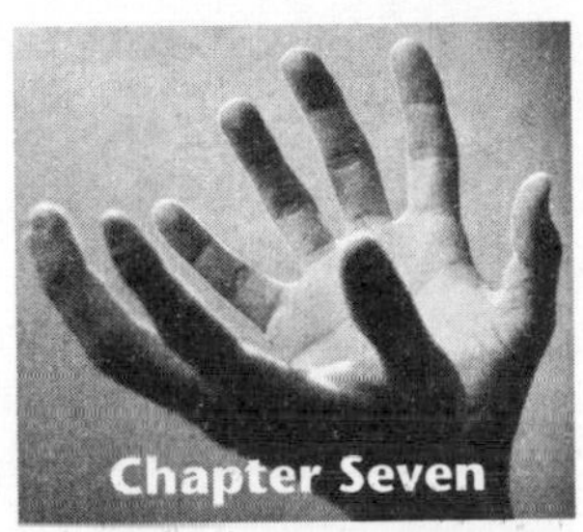

The GLORY of Reconciliation

You couldn't tell by looking at her. A moist palm print on her desktop would have been the only hint of the paralyzing fear that threatened to make her bolt from the classroom. Her furtive glances at the clock only heightened her anxiety. In just a few minutes, the young college student would place herself in harm's way—again.

The year was 1960. The place, Nashville, Tennessee. The young woman was named Diane Nash, a student at Fisk University who had come to the South to escape the restlessness she felt at home. Her fear was unusual, but totally justified. Soon she would join a handful of fellow students and head for the lunch counters in downtown Nashville. Not what you would call a harrowing activity under normal circumstances. But in the 1960s South, there was no such thing as "normal circumstances." You see, Diane and her friends were black. The lunch counters they intended to sit at served only whites. Heckling, racial epithets, burns from hot coffee poured on them, or from cigarettes being extinguished on their heads would be on their "menu." No wonder Diane's palms were sweaty.

As I begin this chapter, I too, feel moisture gathering on my palms. Why? Because some issues still cause us to flinch. Some topics, like racism—in the church or in society at large—get us all wound up and we begin either passionately defending all the strides we've made in race relations, or vehemently blasting away at all the inequalities and injustices that still remain.

I know I put myself at risk by addressing this issue. When I mentioned the topic of this chapter to a respected college professor and pastor friend of mine, he smiled sardonically and said, "You know, it's much easier to write about prayer!" I knew exactly what he meant. I can't tell you how tempted I was to drop this chapter from the book. Writing in the March/April 1999 issue of *PRINT*, Leigh Ann Steer said, "Race relations can be such a touchy subject that it often seems best avoided altogether, with work tailored to keep race from being an issue. But don't be fooled: Not thinking about race is frequently where trouble begins; race permeates everything in some fashion."

In other words, as long as you stick to certain generic topics, you're OK. But if you touch a part of the corporate anatomy that is bruised and tender—if you go to meddling—you're at risk for being misunderstood and misjudged.

If our faith doesn't challenge us on those areas that touch us at the core of our being, it isn't worth much.

But if our faith doesn't challenge us on those areas that touch us at the core of our being, it isn't worth much. It certainly isn't "revival faith." And I believe with all my heart that a revived church will be a racially reconciled church. I dare to believe, as did pastor C.M. Kinney, the first African-

American to be ordained to the gospel ministry in the Seventh-day Adventist church, that the "Third Angel's Message has the power in it to eliminate (or) remove this race prejudice upon the part of those who get hold of the 'truth.'"[1] This is my dream for the church. A church united, diverse, strong.

The way we were

I was told a story about a group of black singers who were invited to sing special music at a large white church. When the singers arrived they slipped in quietly so as not to disrupt the program. Soon they were approached by an usher and were asked to move to the rear of the church. The musicians stated that they were the special music that morning, hoping that once the usher realized they were fellow Adventists, the request would be dropped. To the shock and humiliation of these young people, the usher dismissed what they said and threatened to call the deacons to forcibly remove them. Once settled into their roped-off section, it is said that the pastor's wife smiled at them and said, "We love you; we just don't want to sit with you."

Though we recoil in horror today, hardly believing that incidents like this ever occurred in Adventist churches, they did happen—with enough frequency that the only recourse for black Adventists was to form their own conferences. Sadly, the pastor I quoted from above, was ordained without the presence of his own black church members.[2] His ordination in 1887 took place at one of those camp meetings where dark-skinned believers in the Third Angel's Message were not allowed to attend with their white-skinned brothers and sisters.

"Coloreds were terribly mistreated by some of the White Seventh-day Adventists who at the same time were teaching about the coming of the Lord and the end time. Segregation of the races was reaching an all time high."[3]

Perhaps one of the lowest moments for the church occurred during the Civil Rights movement when it failed to show the world something different. Segregation was "politically correct" in the middle decades of the 20th century, and the Christian community, mimicking their Jewish forerunners who bowed before Nebuchadnezzar's golden image, embraced the idol of prejudice and failed to be God's contemporary Shadrach, Meshach, or Abednego, and stand up for love.

Prophetically speaking, John the Revelator pointed forward to the opening of the seventh seal when "there was silence in heaven about the space of half an hour"(Revelation 8:1, KJV). But this silence had no correlation with the nearly 400-year silence that has come from the Christian church concerning the race issue—a silence that is deafening and disappointing.

In his famous letter from Birmingham jail, Dr. King wrote of his disappointment with the white clergymen who criticized the Civil Rights movement and opted to maintain the status quo.

> *I must honestly reiterate that I have been disappointed with the church . . . . too many have been more cautious than courageous and have remained silent behind the anesthetizing security of stained-glass windows. . . . I have wept over the laxity of the church. But be assured that my tears have been tears of love. There can be no deep disappointment where there is not deep love. . . . Yes, I see the church as the body of Christ. But, oh! How we have blemished and scarred that body through social neglect and through fear of being nonconformists.*[4]

This repugnant silence was forced upon members of this church who offered positive solutions to the segregation problem. Consider what happened to the black evangelist J.G. Thomas, who shared a concept for colored conferences while riding with his state president. "The president stopped the car and threatened to put him out if he made the statement again. In 1929 when mention was made of colored conferences, the leaders were told to 'be silent on this matter and never to mention it again until Jesus comes.'"[5]

Then there was G. E. Peters, who served as director of the Negro Department. During an administrative committee meeting, he was asked to offer a prayer and blessing over the food when the group recessed for lunch. "Peters noted to his colleagues that it was interesting that 'we can pray together, but we cannot eat together. I will be happy when we can get colored conferences.' The chairman of the meeting, W.B. Otis, immediately grabbed him by the collar, shook him and commanded that he 'never mention such again.'"[6]

Love,* not *the Sabbath is the "greatest commandment," and will identify His people as being uniquely His.

For me, the checkered past of our church on race relations is most perplexing. Doctrinally, this church has always found the courage to go against the flow. The Sabbath, the State of the Dead, the Sanctuary message, etc., were all teachings that distinguished our movement from mainstream Christendom. The stigma of proclaiming minority or "errant" views has never caused us to capitulate. But when it came to the issue of race—the issue of love—the remnant church stopped being a "peculiar people" and shamefully conformed to the popular thinking of the day. And we all know which of the two—doctrine or love—Jesus said would set His people apart. Love, *not* the Sabbath, was the "greatest commandment," and would identify His people as being uniquely His. (See John 13:35.)

The stresses of the present

I read with shock a newsletter published by a group of ministers advocating the formation of a new regional (black) conference in my home state. What shocked me was not the argument in favor of such a move, but the venomous tone of the supporters. Ordained men of God hurled scathing taunts and sarcastic jabs at fellow members who didn't see the issue the way they did. It was offensive and, again, very disappointing.

Unfortunately for all of us, the silence and denials from one segment of the church has sown the seeds of distrust and anger from another segment of the church. I had to acknowledge the truth behind the words of Chris Rice, managing editor of *Urban Family* magazine, when he wrote: "A new virus of 'separate but equal' is invading the national bloodstream: all-black suburbs, fast-growing churches that deliver on their promise of an 'Afrocentric' experience, and blacks-only college dorms. The message is, 'Give us our piece of the pie, and get out of our face.'

"This backlash is often the painful cry of a wronged race. Sometimes it is the voice of a new form of black racism, where black is always beautiful and white is never right. Either way, the result is separation, distrust, and intimidation of anyone, white or black, who challenges the blacks-only emphasis with a higher ideal."[7]

Why now, at the dawn of a new century, do we still find a need to separate along racial lines? Have we not grown or learned anything over the last 30-50 years? At the risk of sounding naive, I believe God wants us to do and be better! Even as the hardness of men's hearts made divorce a necessary evil, the hardness and cowardice of our hearts in the early years of the twentieth century necessitated the formation of black conferences. And though Satan may have meant it for evil, God has worked marvelously through these institutions to minister effectively to African Americans.

"Today, some of the most productive units of the denomination are the 'Regional Conferences' in the North American Division of the World Church, representing 27.08 percent of the membership in the United States and contributing 20.12 percent of the tithe for its operation."[8]

No one, least of all me who was born on the West Coast, will minimize the glorious history and contributions made by black-led institutions. But in the 21st century, should we still be calling for organizational structures that remind us of our lack of submission to God and to each other? When, if not now on the eve of Christ's return, will we begin to call for and *insist* on a church that reflects the kingdom we are about to inherit? If we can't or won't deal with the pride and prejudices that keep us apart, we are fooling ourselves about revival or receiving latter rain power. God *will* have a different people on the face of the earth, and it must begin with you and me—members of the revival generation.

If we can't or won't deal with the pride and prejudices that keep us apart, we are fooling ourselves about revival or receiving latter rain power.

Yes, we still have churches in cities where the White Adventists have no idea what's going on in the Black Adventist churches. I've preached in predominantly White churches for so-called "city-wide" prayer conferences where the Black Adventists were markedly absent. When I probed further, I discovered that the information didn't get out, or that proper "protocol" wasn't followed. And the reverse is also true. C'mon church. Wake up! Please!

Do you know how embarrassing it is to try to explain to new members why we have separate conferences? What message are we sending? And lest you think I am limiting this discussion to just Black/White relationships, think again. The power struggles between Caribbean Blacks and American Blacks; between Mexican Americans and South Americans; between Dominicans and Haitians; Hutu and Tutsi are legendary and deep.

My friends, our religion is insufficient to transform us. Religion never transforms. Only *relationship* with Jesus Christ makes us new people inside and out.

Without a committed relationship to Christ where He is the supreme theme of our faith, we choose culture over confession, ethnicity above ethics, and race ahead of religion. In an impassioned sermon given at the Seabrook SDA Church, November 22, 1997, Pastor Wintley Phipps made this startling statement: "For many Christians who say the supreme theme of their faith is Jesus Christ, often they don't know themselves, and they don't realize that the supreme theme of their faith is *not* Christ. . . . And they will only know it when they come to a crisis."[9]

This is exactly what happened in Rwanda during the genocide of 1994. This highly Christianized nation was ripped apart by bloody intertribal warfare. Many believers in the Three Angels' Messages were hacked to death by fellow believers who happened to belong to the rival tribe.

How could this happen? What was the cause of such a flagrant disregard of Christian love and brotherhood? Because we settled for a gospel strong enough to save but too weak to reconcile! Because we didn't allow the message of the new birth to transform us into new creatures (see 2 Corinthians 5:17). Because, in a crisis, the true foundational belief system came to the surface and it wasn't Christ, it was tribal loyalty.

Many great revivalists of the past—men I respect, admire, and have quoted in this book—also failed to be fully transformed by the revivals they led. "Some of the noted New England leaders who endorsed this perspective of slavery were George Whitefield, John Davenport, Ever Styles, and Jonathan Edwards. They attempted to teach the slaves to docilely accept their inferior status, for to do so was the will of God. To fail to do so was to rebel against God and risk eternal punishment."[10]

Inexplicably, these great men of faith, as have others since them, adopted a "skin-deep" revival that believed it is possible to be reconciled to God without being reconciled to your neighbor. "Whenever Christians have accommodated that fallacy," says Chris Rice, "it has spelled disaster for the world, whether in the form of 'born-again' slaveholders, hymn-singing Holocaust engineers, or Scripture-quoting apartheid supporters."[11]

But true revival—the revival that transforms and penetrates to the bone and marrow of who we are—is an all or nothing proposition. "Revival comes from heaven when heroic souls enter the conflict determined to win or die," writes Charles Finney, "or if need be, to win and die!"

I want an all-on-the-altar faith, don't you? I don't want my witness compromised by fears and prejudices that I reserve the right to justify based on how I'm treated. I don't want to be a Christian only when it's politically correct, convenient, and comfortable. I want a Christianity that does what's right all the time.

Here's the bottom line: if separation and suspicion is the best we can do, we'd better drop the remnant label right now and settle for something far more humble. In this we are not "peculiar," we are like the world around us not "called out," but just like everyone else. My dream is that we recapture our distinctiveness and truly strive to be something unique on the face of the earth.

We must learn to love and trust each other, for this will surely be the greatest evidence of a true Holy Ghost revival among us.

At a potluck dinner in Connecticut, I was talking with a gentleman who had heard me address the "R" word in my sermon. He described some of the battles that were taking place at that moment in his conference headquarters. He looked me in the eye and said, "Do you really believe things can ever change?"

"I *have* to believe that," I replied. "Or else I'd have to admit that there was something too big and deep for God to handle. And I'm not prepared to say that, are you?"

I agree with J. Anthony Boger who pastors the multicultural

Westminster Good Samaritan Church in Westminster, California. He said, "If we fail to believe that the 'impossible' is, in fact, possible through the power of God, then we need to stop calling ourselves the church. It is time to shake up the status quo, which is often rooted in the meaningless traditions that have divided us."[12]

I'm not saying it's going to be easy, but we've all got to start somewhere. And I don't really care who makes the first move. When the Spirit says, "Move," *move!* When He says, "Come together," *come together!* When He says "Reconcile," *reconcile!* For Christ's sake, we must learn to trust *and* love each other, *for this will surely be the greatest evidence of a true Holy Ghost revival among us. Not baptisms, but brotherhood. Not an increase in tithe, but an increase of trust.*

So how do we begin?

Admit our problem

Some of us have been raised with certain racial prejudices. Stop pretending. Admit it before God and confess the negative stereotypes that you've allowed to keep you from developing meaningful relationships with members of a different ethnic group.

I'll never forget how I felt when a co-worker of mine at Pacific Press voluntarily told me of his racist upbringing, and how he now realizes how wrong he was for some of the things he used to say and feel towards minorities. With tears in his eyes, he asked my forgiveness. What an example of true revival! I was overwhelmed and though I was unaware of his past and had enjoyed friendly relations with him to that point, our friendship was deepened by this cleansing exchange.

Begin to explore

How many people unlike yourself form your inner circle? How willing are you to cross over into unfamiliar territory and develop a friendship with somebody who is different? Take steps to enter someone else's world.

Go home with them after church. Get on their turf. Be in places where you might not be as comfortable, but where you will have a chance to see how your friend lives and what their world is like.

Read literature, periodicals, or view films about/by other ethnic groups

Gary is one of my closest friends. When my family moved to Idaho, he and his family showed an immediate interest in us. Our daughters became fast friends and remain so to this day. Gary is not shy and wanted to know about Black heritage and wanted insight into some of the struggles of our people. Our talks were often frank and pointed. But it wasn't until he bought the six-part video documentary series called *Eyes on the Prize: America's Civil Rights Years*, and watched it with his children, that he began to understand the struggle and pain of African-Americans. I'll let him tell it in his own words:

I have a friend who I have a lot of respect for, and whose association has greatly benefited my life. We had long talked about going to one of his prayer conferences together, and here we were. He, the guest speaker, and I the tag along. I viewed my roll as that of a prayer warrior, praying quietly in the background for my friend as he spoke. While this was what I felt I was there to do, there was something else in the back of my mind.

Two years prior to this, my friend and I were working together with some other men on a men's conference for our church. We had been discussing various topics—reconciliation among them. I had recently attended a Promise Keepers workshop and listened to a Hispanic man tell us how privileged we whites were, and that we were responsible for the suppression of minorities. I was offended. I felt that he had just used the platform of Promise Keepers for his own personal "white bashing." I felt the attendees were there to grow in the

Lord, but this was one more attempt to blame everything on us white males.

So, when the topic of reconciliation came up in our meeting, I expressed my feelings and basically excused myself from any personal responsibility for reconciliation, and offered my "clean record" on the subject as the justification. Unfortunately, my outspoken personality is such that I don't always fully analyze the full effects of what I am saying before I open my mouth. It was then I noticed the look of pain in my friend's eyes.

The second time I saw that look was in the aftermath of the Waco tragedy. I was reacting to the governmental siege and ultimate burning of the Branch Davidian compound saying, "Not in my United States! This really can't be happening in my United States. This is not the way we do things here." I felt violated and hurt to see what was happening. My friend said that this was the way he felt about the race issue in this country.

As I pondered his remark and remembered the look on his face months earlier, the Lord spoke to my heart, impressing me of my need to gain more understanding. I read a book on reconciliation. That was good, but I still felt it was kind of phony for me to accept responsibility for the actions of others. Then I watched an excellent series called "Eyes on the Prize," *a documentary on the civil rights movement. As I watched that series, with tears in my eyes, I kept saying "Not in my United States. We didn't do that here, did we? Do we? It was after that that the Lord opened up my heart to the need for me to express my deep sorrow for what is and has happened to my black brothers.*

We are all part of the body of Christ. Whatever healing needs to take place is my responsibility because of love. His love for me, His love for you, and our love for each other.

Tearfully, my friend embraced me and committed himself to the ministry of reconciliation that God gave the church. I, too, am committed to the same ministry. We have had the privilege of traveling together and speaking out on the issue of racial healing. Hearts have been deeply stirred as people witnessed reconciliation in "living color."

But it begins with understanding. Visit the library, get your hands on literature from other ethnic groups. Get a fresh perspective on the passions, experiences, struggles and dreams of those outside your own circle. As you do this, walls of ignorance and misunderstanding will begin to crumble.

Bring in speakers of different ethnic backgrounds

As I said earlier, it is not uncommon in large urban centers for there to be no interaction whatsoever between churches of different cultural backgrounds—even if they are of the same denomination! These church members preach the same doctrine, pray to the same God, and pay tithe to the same institutional storehouse. But the cultural divide prevents them from enjoying fellowship with each other.

One way to break through this barrier is to encourage your pastor to arrange a swapping of pulpits with the pastor of a church of another ethnic makeup. Hold joint services that involve different worship styles. Allow yourself to be blessed by the nuances and fresh perspectives the other group brings to your understanding of God. Get out of your "box" and rub shoulders with this new breed of people called the Body of Christ. It'll change you.

Join together for prayer

As I mentioned in chapter five, many churches have begun to come together for what is called "the concert of prayer." The idea is for churches within the same city or geographical area to conduct joint prayer meetings for the purpose of seeking revival in their churches and communities. I spoke at a city-wide prayer conference in Memphis, Tennessee two years ago where several Black churches came together and committed themselves to this concert of prayer model. When I suggested including the White churches, the idea was met with great skepticism. The Black pastors had little confidence that their White counterparts would be willing to participate in a program that was initiated by non-Whites. We prayed about it. Approximately six months later I encountered one of the Black pastors from Memphis who told me that the concert of prayer was convening regularly once a month and that new churches—including White churches—were joining the effort. If we can just start praying together, there is no force on earth that can stop God's people from being united.

Start now

Be assured that the enemy wants to keep Christians weak, separate, and racially divided. Is it easier to stay within our own comfort zones? You bet. Is it hard work to enter into someone else's world and try to see life from their perspective? Yes. Is it difficult to develop long-term friendships with someone of a different ethnic group? Perhaps. But is it the will of God that we love one another as Christ has loved us? Yes. In fact, it is our Savior's commandment (see John 15:12, 17).

"Christianity doesn't require any power when its only challenge is doing something that already comes naturally," wrote Spencer Perkins. "But it will take a powerful gospel—a gospel with guts—to enable us to love across all the barriers we erect to edify our own kind and protect us from our insecurities."[13]

Christianity doesn't require any power when its only challenge is doing something that already comes naturally.

In the process of establishing new friendships, be honest. Don't be phony. Ask real questions. Risk appearing stupid. Be willing to hear the good, the bad, and the ugly things that have transpired between members of different cultural groups. Study the Scriptures together and look for opportunities, such as festivals or performances, that celebrate your own culture as well as others.

Reconciliation Generation

In an April 1996 editorial, *Adventist Review* editor William G. Johnsson observed the plague of Black church burnings that were leaving a smoldering blot of hatred on the American landscape. He asked a question followed by a plea that I think we would all do well to answer.

> *Will we capitulate to culture, or will we confront culture when culture opposes the gospel? Too often we have succumbed to culture. I have lived on three continents and have seen it, have been a part of it. I confess it with shame: racist attitudes toward the Aboriginal people of my native Australia, caste considerations in India, Black-White animosity in North America. God help us to confront the culture! God help us all to confront our racism! God help us to bring our need out in the open!*[14]

Who will take up Christ's banner of unity and begin to live according to His "New World Order"—where there is neither Jew nor Greek, bond nor free, male nor female, but we are all one in Him (see Gal. 3:28)? The revival generation will.

As I write this, our church has just concluded a leadership summit on race relations, in answer to President Clinton's call for the faith community to take the lead in this area. The theme for the summit was "Racial Harmony in the New Millennium: Making it happen." More than 300 church administrators and institutional leaders were invited to take part in a dialogue from which would emerge bold initiatives for dismantling racism, and on-going mechanisms to continually motivate, expand, and monitor the progress of those initiatives. I applaud this effort and pray that we will be "the head and not the tail" on pioneering a kingdom-based model of reconciliation in keeping with our high calling. But it will take courage, *prayer*, perseverance, *prayer*, humility, *prayer*, forgiveness, *prayer*, and PRAYER to make it happen!

The revival generation is a *reconciliation* generation and will stand out from the crowd because of their uncompromising commitment to represent "kingdom culture" and embrace Christ as the supreme theme of their faith. In contrast to the church of the 20th century—the one Dr. King called the "arch defender of the status quo" and "a thermometer that recorded the ideas and principles of popular opinion," this generation of believers will be a thermostat that transforms the mores of society. This generation will not shrink from the difficult task of reconciliation, but rather it will derive strength from its brokenness as Blacks and Whites, Asians and Hispanics come together to confess and confront, to bless and to pray.

The revival generation represents only one kingdom and they will stand at last united—proud of their respective heritage and radiant with the gifts inherent in their diverse cultures. Yet they stand under only one banner—the blood-stained banner of the Lamb slain from the foundation of the world. Here we stand. We can do no other!

◆ ◆ ◆

A prayer

Lord, forgive me for where I have failed to love my brother as You do.
Forgive my petty prejudices and the grudges I've justified because of how I've been treated or how I was raised.
I have claimed citizenship in the kingdom of heaven were love reigns, but have lived according to the social mores of the kingdom of earth where racism reigns. Forgive my duplicity, Lord.
Give me the courage to reflect Your heart and reject my own.

Give me the strength to forgive and to ask forgiveness of those I've hurt or neglected. Let me not be so quick to defend my "goodness" because it is all as filthy rags in Your eyes. Thank You for Your grace that covers my nakedness, help me to extend that same grace to others.
Amen.

---

[1] Charles E. Deadly, Sr., *Thou Who Hath Brought Us...* (Burton, N.Y.: TEACH Services, Inc., 1997), 163.
[2] *Ibid.*, p. 161.
[3] *Ibid.*, p. 161.
[4] Martin Luther King, Jr., "Letter From Birmingham Jail," April 16, 1963, Internet: http://www.msstate.edu/Archives/History/USA/Afro-American/birmingham.king
[5] Charles E. Deadly, Sr., *Thou Who Hath Brought Us...*, p. 165.
[6] *Ibid.*, p. 166.
[7] Chris Rice, "By This All Men Will Know," *Discipleship Journal*, issue eighty-seven, 1995, p. 77.
[8] *Thou Who Hath Brought Us...*, p. 166.
[9] Wintley Phipps in recorded message entitled, "The Supreme Theme of Your Faith," Seabrook SDA Church, November 22, 1997.
[10] Tony Evans, *Let's Get to Know Each Other* (Nashville: Thomas Nelson Publishers, 1995), 8.
[11] Chris Rice, "By This All Men Will Know," *Discipleship Journal*, issue eighty-seven, 1995, p. 75.
[12] J. Anthony Boger, "Not Really A 'Miracle' Church," *Ministry*, July 1999, p. 21.
[13] Spencer Perkins, "Who Is My Neighbor?" *Discipleship Journal*, issue eighty-seven, 1995, p. 80.
[14] William G. Johnsson, "As Churches Burn," *Adventist Review*, April 1996, p. 5.

We never become truly spiritual
by sitting down and wishing to become so.
You must undertake something so great
that you cannot accomplish it unaided.
–Phillips Brooks

Anyone can devise a plan by which good people go to heaven.
Only God can devise a plan whereby sinners,
which are His enemies, can go to heaven.
–Lewis Sperry Chafer

" 'Is anything too hard for the Lord?' "
–Genesis 18:14

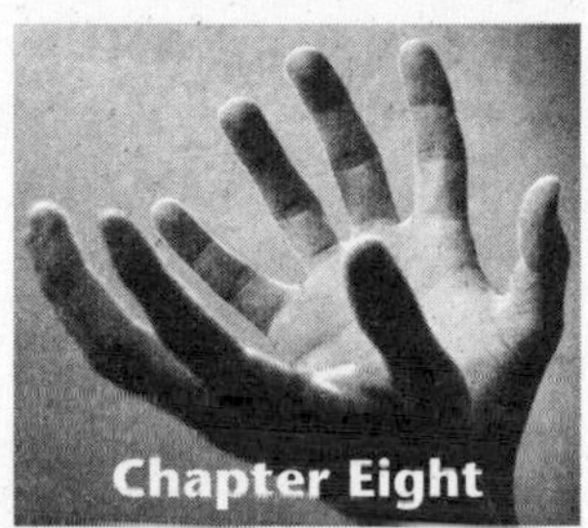

The GLORY of the Impossible

God loves "impossible" things. Maybe that explains why He's so in love with the church. Because from all outward appearances, it seems impossible that the church will ever be like the Savior she claims to follow.

It was G. K. Chesterton who said, "Christianity has not been tried and found wanting. It has been found difficult and left untried." Apparently, when considering the behavior of many Christians, Chesterton was confronted with a contradiction of profession and practice. A contradiction that remains to this day.

I will confess to you that there are times when I look at myself and my church and I think, *Like Christ? Fat chance!* Remember that quotation I cited in the introduction? "Christ is waiting with longing desire for the manifestation of Himself in His church. When the character of Christ shall be perfectly reproduced in His people, then He will come to claim them as His own."[1] This statement leaves me scratching my head and wondering if a childhood head wound caused Mrs. White to suffer a temporary blackout when she made it.

5—B.B.G.

I mean no disrespect, but how can this be possible? "Lord," I say, "how can my generation possibly be the generation to perfectly reproduce your character? Have you looked at us lately? We're too tired, too distracted, too self-centered, too busy, too shallow, to reproduce your character."

Doesn't it appear that way to you? Weren't there other generations more suited to the task? What about the early 18th century during the "Great Awakening" when Jonathan Edwards was setting New England ablaze with the gospel and witnessing hundreds of conversions to Christ? Or when George Whitefield and John Wesley were pursuing sinners "like men storming a beach." Observing these men, J. C. Ryle was quoted as saying, "The role was reversed: all heaven was let loose upon Britain in 1739."[2] What about the early 1800s when William Miller, Joseph Bates, and Josiah Litch had Christians everywhere ready to meet the Lord?

These giants of faith didn't have cable, DVD, cell phones, Palm Pilots, PCs, CD players, Nintendo, fax machines, or the Internet to distract them. They were deep Bible students, more likely to weep for the lost than to fume about getting out of church after noon!

So why now? Why our generation? Because God loves to use the "foolish things of the world to shame the wise." He gets a kick out of choosing "the weak things of the world to shame the strong." It makes His day to use "the things that are not—to nullify the things that are." Why? "So that no one may boast before him" (1 Corinthians 1:27-29). When God does impossible things, there's no mistaking Who gets the credit! And when He pulls off the impossible stunt of reproducing His character in *this* Laodicean generation, He will get all the glory!

God of the impossible

Perhaps the greatest revival that ever took place was not initiated through a man named Roberts, Wesley, or Finney. No, the greatest revival took place in a bone yard through a man named Ezekiel.

Ezekiel was called to the prophetic office five years after he and 10,000

Jews were exiled to Babylon. Zedekiah succeeded Jehoiachin as King of Judah, but in his 11th year (586 B.C.), Judah was finally overthrown. The remnant of the people were taken, the temple burned, and Jerusalem destroyed. The surviving captives and exiles were utterly defeated and hopelessly depressed. Psalm 137:1-6 expresses their inconsolable grief at the loss of their homeland and God's favor.

> *By the rivers of Babylon,*
> *There we sat down and wept,*
> *When we remembered Zion.*
> *Upon the willows in the midst of it*
> *We hung our harps.*
> *For there our captors demanded of us songs,*
> *And our tormentors mirth, saying,*
> *"Sing us one of the songs of Zion."*
> *How can we sing the Lord's song*
> *In a foreign land? (NASB)*

Can't you hear their depression? It's like a huge sigh. They had lost their homes, their identity, their freedom, and their song. With sadistic glee, their Babylonian captors mocked the Jews by asking them to "Sing us one of the songs of Zion." But the harps had been hung on the willows. There could be no singing of the Lord's songs in a foreign land.

The exiled Hebrews had a proverbial saying that pervaded their conversation. "Our bones are dried up, and our hope is perished. We are completely cut off." Perhaps this saying was rolling around in Ezekiel's mind at the time of this vision.

What made matters worse were the reports coming from the home front—Jerusalem—of a horrific final battle in which the fallen warriors had the flesh flayed from their bones, and the bones were left to dry in the hot sun. This news was almost too much. These were their fathers, husbands, and sons! If the reports were true, this was a disaster of unparalleled proportions.

But for Ezekiel, an even greater grief was the spiritual deadness of his people. The exiles had become the dead among the living. And this is always the case when hope is lost. Whenever our capacity to hope is extinguished, we are among the living dead. Whenever our love for God and others grows cold and perfunctory, the Lord says, "You are dead, dry, defeated, deadly dull."

Aren't you glad He doesn't stop there? God doesn't leave us in our hopelessness. Spiritually, we may be oh so dead, but that's where the fun begins! That's when God struts His stuff! The Hebrews may have been the dead among the living, but what God wanted Ezekiel to witness was *how* He would make them the living among the dead! He wanted Ezekiel and He wants us to know that when it comes to revival, " 'What is impossible with men is possible with God' " (Luke 18:27).

The rest of the story

The 37th chapter of Ezekial transports us to a valley full of bones. The bones are described as being "very dry" (v. 2). No doubt these bones had been there a long time. Such piles of human bones were not unknown in the ancient world. After bloody battles, the victorious army would bury their dead. The defeated army, however, often left their dead on the field of battle. The corpses would be left there to humiliate the conquered.

Who can forget the civil war and famine crisis in Somalia in the early 90s? This African nation had succumbed to a famine that would, along with the fighting, eventually kill 350,000 people. U.S. and U.N. troops were sent to bring stability to the region, but what started out as a humanitarian relief mission to the starving Somali people, became a war between the U.S. and self-proclaimed president and warlord Muhammed Farrah Aidid. It proved to be a no-win confrontation for the U.S. that ended in the loss of 30 American lives, including that of a U.S. soldier whose battered body was dragged through the streets of Mogadishu to complete America's humiliation.

This detestable treatment of a fallen U.S. soldier was reminiscent of the treatment the dead received in Ezekiel's time. The goal was embarrassment and intimidation. The armies of Israel had fallen before Babylon and the massive piles of bones were a grotesque reminder to all who saw them of Babylon's decisive triumph.

The Lord takes Ezekiel on a walking tour among the bones. If you're American, you remember how you felt when you saw that U.S. soldier's body dragged through the streets? Then you can imagine what Ezekiel must have been feeling as this vision of dry bones unfolded before him. Suddenly, The Lord asks Ezekiel *the* question. " 'Son of man, **can these bones live?**' " (v. 3, emphasis added.)

I've said it once, and I'll say it again, the Lord asks some incredible questions! To Abraham, the question was "Can your 90-year-old wife get pregnant?" To Moses, it was "Can the sea open and your people cross on dry land?" To Elijah, "Can fire come down from heaven in answer to prayer?" To the disciples, "Can you feed 5,000 with a sack lunch?" And to Mary and Martha the question was "Can your brother, who has been dead for four days, come back to life?"

The obvious answer to all of these questions is *No*. These are, humanly speaking, *impossibilities*. These are problems beyond the reach of man. I once heard pastor T.D. Jakes say that if you've got a problem a man can solve, you haven't got a problem. By that definition, Ezekiel is facing a *real* problem.

"Can these bones live, Ezekiel?" The obvious answer is *No*. But somewhere in the back of Ezekiel's mind, he recalls hearing about a shaft of flame that vaporized a water-logged bullock on Mt. Carmel. Somewhere in the inner recesses of Ezekiel's consciousness he remembers hearing about a highway through the Red Sea. And somewhere buried deep in his mental database, Ezekiel remembers a 90-year-old woman with morning sickness.

If you've got a problem a man can solve, you haven't got a problem.

Suddenly Ezekiel becomes aware of *Who* is asking the question. And in this moment of insight, the bewildered prophet remembers yet another of God's incredible questions: " '*Is anything too hard for the Lord?*' " (Genesis 18:14.)

Ezekiel's hesitation

But instead of a resounding *Yes!* Ezekiel balks. There's a moment of hesitation. Ezekiel wrestles between what he *believes* by faith and what he *sees* with his eyes. Like the song the children sing, Ezekiel believes "My God is so big, my God is so mighty, there's nothing my God cannot do," yet he's looking at something overwhelmingly impossible.

You've been there, haven't you? I know I have. Our faith tells us one thing and our eyes see another.

We *believe* God provided manna in the wilderness; but we *see* the pink slip in our hands and face the unemployment line.

We *believe* God resurrected Lazarus from the dead, but we *see* a family torn apart by divorce, or the casket of a loved one lowered into the earth.

We *believe* God healed the lepers and cast out demons, but we *see* the x-rays from the doctor that don't look good, and *feel* the psychological wounds from abusive pasts.

Oh yes, we understand Ezekiel's hesitation. We understand when he sidesteps God's question and goes for a non-committal " 'O Sovereign Lord, you alone know' " (Ezekiel 37:3).

Will your prodigal son or daughter eventually turn to Christ and be saved? Will the judge suspend your child's sentence? Will the remission hold? Will your wife ever come home again? Will you ever get the promotion you deserve? Will the church you're a part of ever stop its death-spiral and find new life in Jesus? Our faith wants to say Yes, but our eyes say No, and our mouths respond as Ezekiel's: "O Lord, You know! I believe, help Thou my unbelief!"

The next time you're surveying the dry bones in your life, spiritually stuck between belief and circumstance, between what you can and cannot see, and the stalemate is causing you to wither and die inside, remember these three commands of the Lord. This is how God revives dry bones.

1. Speak the Word of the Lord.

Note the instructions God gives to Ezekiel in verse 4: "'Then he said to me, 'Prophesy to these bones and say to them . . .' " Generally speaking, do people talk to bones? Not usually. (Unless a wife tries to speak to her husband or children when they're watching TV. Then it's like talking to a *wall.*) This is just a little strange. But we serve a "strange" and wonderful God whose thoughts are not our thoughts, and whose ways are not our ways. " 'As the heavens are higher than the earth, so are my ways higher than your ways and my thoughts than your thoughts' " (Isaiah 55:9).

The word for *prophesy* in Hebrew is **naba** (*naw baw*) a prime root meaning "to speak (or sing) by inspiration (in prediction or simple discourse)." I believe God wants us to be encouragers—to speak (or prophesy) words of hope, life and comfort to the hurting and helpless. Too many of our churches are being ruined by critical tongues, and God forgive me, I've wagged my own tongue in criticism too many times. This must stop.

Much of the dryness we experience in our churches will begin to heal when the spirit of criticism is replaced by the spirit of encouragement. "Do not let any unwholesome talk come out of your mouths," said the Apostle Paul, "but only what is helpful for building others up according to their needs, that it may benefit those who listen" (Ephesians 4:29).

Much of the dryness we experience in our churches will begin to heal when the spirit of criticism is replaced by the spirit of encouragement.

Imagine how this would transform the church! Speak the Word of God to people. Speak about Christ. Dwell on His promises and His love. Don't encourage discouragement. Don't give way to gossip or doubt.

> *Every word of doubt you utter is inviting Satan's temptations; it is strengthening in you the tendency to doubt . . . If you talk out your feelings, every doubt you express not only reacts upon yourself, but it is a seed that will germinate and bear fruit in the life of others, and it may be impossible to counteract the influence of your words. . . How important that we speak only those things that will give spiritual strength and life!* [3]

We need to pray, *Lord, put Your words in my mouth that I may encourage someone today.*

2. "Hear the Word of the Lord" (Verse 4)

After the command to speak to the bones, the bones are told to "hear the word of the Lord!" Bones don't generally hear well do they? But when God speaks water parts, fire falls, corpses dance, and bones listen!

Please take note that only two things brought these bones to life: **God's word and God's spirit.** Nothing else. Nothing of man. Nothing of Ezekiel. Nothing of the bones. This is ample evidence that we need the Word of God today as never before! Sadly, as noted in chapter two, the unadulterated Word of God is becoming rare.

The world is perishing for want of the gospel. There is a famine for the word of God. There are few who preach the word unmixed with human tradition. Though men have the Bible in their hands, they do not receive the blessing that God has placed in it for them.[4]

Perhaps we would get more out of God's Word if we started *living* it. At a recent Essence Awards program, gospel artist Kirk Franklin said this when accepting his award: "We write songs that degrade our women and praise God for the awards we win . . . It's time we stopped preaching Christ and started walking Christ." Profession without practice is meaningless. Hearing without doing is equally empty.

Hearing and doing are synonymous to the Jewish mind. "Be ye doers of the word," says James, "and not hearers only, deceiving your own selves" (James 1:22, KJV). If you don't act on what God is saying to you, you fall into the worst kind of deception. Think of all the sermons you've heard, Sabbath School classes you've attended, and religious tapes you've listened to over the years. If Christians acted on one-third of all they've heard, the world and our churches would be radically different places! Actually putting God's Word into practice is the hard part, but oh, how we *love* to debate it! We can study and argue and wax eloquent with the best of them, but, as Andrew Murray said,

The knowledge that occupies and pleases and at length satisfies the mind, without day-by-day leading to the faith, the actions, the character, and the true inner life for which God meant it, is the most dangerous of all enemies.[5]

Ezekiel himself had to contend with a "hearers only" congregation. In chapter 33, God shows Ezekiel this hindrance to revival among his people.

> *As for you, son of man, your countrymen are talking together about you by the walls and at the doors of the houses, saying to each other, "Come and hear the message that has come from the Lord." My people come to you, as they usually do, and sit before you to listen to your words, but THEY DO NOT PUT THEM INTO PRACTICE. With their mouths they express devotion, but their hearts are greedy for unjust gain. Indeed, to them you are nothing more than one who sings love songs with a beautiful voice and plays an instrument well, for THEY HEAR YOUR WORDS BUT DO NOT PUT THEM INTO PRACTICE* (vs. 30-32, emphasis added.)

Doesn't this sound like a lot of Christians today? People "church hop," bouncing around from church to church in search of the best "show" in town. "Who's preaching at your church today? Oh, I've heard her already!" "Where's such and such a group performing?" "I hear Pastor so and so is coming to town!"

Ezekiel had become the hottest preacher in Babylon! His popularity soared after Jerusalem's fall, for his warnings had all come true. Even so, his audience listened just for entertainment, as they would to music. This danger still exists today. Jim Cymbala, pastor of the renowned Brooklyn Tabernacle, says, "Preaching itself can easily become just a subtle form of entertainment."[6]

God reminds us through this passage that the true purpose of prophecy is to change people's lives, not to draw a crowd. "Many delude themselves into thinking that by observing they are part of something interesting and exciting and productive," writes Douglas Cooper, "while actually they do and accomplish nothing"[7]

I can't tell you what you should do in relation to hearing the Word, but I want you to commit to finding out from God yourself. Is God asking you to identify where you're out of line with His Word so you can confess it and adjust your course? Is God asking you to begin a scripture memory program? Is God asking you to begin praying for Him to show you the action steps to take in specific areas of your life like marriage, or parenting, or your job, or your Christian witness? Is God asking you to change your mental diet and begin a program of systematic reading through the Bible? I don't know, but ask Him how He wants you to change in relation to His Word.

Notice what God says next in verses 5 and 6: " '*I* will make breath . . .*I* will attach tendons . . .[*I* will] make flesh come upon you and cover you . . .*I* will put breath in you, . . .' " (emphasis added.)

Who is doing the action? God. And what is our part? " 'YOU WILL COME TO LIFE.' "

God is always the architect and the builder of life. In the beginning, the world was empty and void, dark and lifeless *until God spoke!* God invaded the darkness and took creative action, replacing the void with light, air, land, grass, planets, animals, and man. He created something out of nothing. And He can enter the black void and emptiness of your greatest fear or struggle and split it wide open with the breath of life. He will do it—all you have to do is be obedient to His Word and live!

3. Talk to God (Pray)

Ezekiel did as he was told, and as he was prophesying these encouraging words of God, "there was a noise, a rattling sound, and the bones came together, bone to bone. I looked, and tendons and flesh appeared on them and skin covered them, . . ." (vs. 7, 8)

Now ask yourself a question: Why didn't the vision end right here? A miracle had just happened, man! Time to break out the chips and salsa. The bones had come together, internal organs and muscles started flying in from all over the place. Flesh covered the bones. What an awesome display of power! Why aren't the credits rolling with the Hallelujah Chorus being sung in the background? *Because as important as the Word of God is, without the Spirit to breathe His life into it and us, we remain spiritually dead!* We are only good-looking corpses.

This is important because you can look good and healthy and prosperous on the outside, and be white-washed tombs full of dead men's bones and everything unclean on the inside (Matthew 23:27). The truth is that the situation only *appeared* to have improved. Before you had bones, now you had corpses, but both are without life.

The most heinous criminals are brought to court all shaved, combed and dressed. They look good. Remember how "cute" the Menendez brothers looked in court? Their lawyer made sure the boys looked like young innocents. But this was a facade. Just beneath the expensive sweaters and Armani suits, beat the hearts of killers. A new suit doesn't change the heart. These corpses still needed life!

As important as the Word of God is,
withouth the Spirit to breathe His life into it and us,
we remain spiritually dead!

Two lessons are to be learned here: (1) Revival takes time. There's a process. First the Word of God is spoken and heard. Next the bones come together, tendons and flesh appear, and finally skin covers them. Spiritual growth takes time. "First the blade, then the ear, after that the full corn in the ear" (Mark 4:28, KJV). Let God finish the work He started in you, and don't bypass the steps to revival along the way. If you try to have Pentecost without Calvary, you will only have the appearance of revival—the glitz but no glory.

(2) Don't stop praying too soon! Don't let go of God until He blesses you.

So God says to Ezekiel " 'Prophesy to the breath; prophesy, son of man, and say to it, "This is what the Sovereign Lord says: Come from the four winds, O breath, and breathe into these slain, that they may live" ' " (v. 9).

The result? "So I prophesied as he commanded me, and breath entered them; they came to life and stood up on their feet—a vast army" (v. 10).

Praise God! What was once a mound of disorganized, disjointed bones, are now standing on their feet—a vast army, ready to fight the battles of the Lord. In the military, when a subordinate wants to tell the commanding officer what's on his heart, he'll say, "permission to speak freely, Sir!" My friends, when it comes to asking the Holy Spirit to bring us to life, we have permission to "speak freely."

> *You are on the earth to carry on my cause. I am in heaven, the Lord of all, the maker of all, the Holy One of all. Now whatever you need for my cause, ask me and I will do it. Shape the future by your prayers, and all that you need for present supplies, command me . . . Ask largely. Open thy mouth wide and I will fill it.* [8]

There are no limits with God. All things are ours through prayer—including and especially revival. Open your mouth wide and ask for it! No matter how impossible it may seem, God is going to bring us to life! If He can bring life to a pile of dry, sun-bleached bones, He can bring back the glory to the altar of my heart and yours. Even now, He is performing a miracle of grace in your life. Even now you are being readied to receive the breath of His Spirit and to take your stand as a soldier in God's loud-cry army.

Soldiers in this army have a different view of life. Not long ago, I received an e-mail entitled, "A Real Soldier's Creed." I don't know who the author is, but I think the sentiments reflect the heart of a child of God who has been resurrected from the bone yard of lukewarm Christianity.

◆ ◆ ◆

A Real SOLDIER's Creed

I am a soldier in the army of my God. The Lord Jesus Christ is my Commanding Officer. The Holy Bible is my code of conduct. Faith,

Prayer and the Word are my weapons of Warfare.

I have been taught by the Holy Spirit, trained by experience, tried by adversity and tested by fire. I am a volunteer in this army, and I am enlisted for eternity. I will either retire in this army at the advent or die in this army; but I will not get out, sell out, be talked out, or pushed out.

I am faithful, reliable, capable and dependable. If my God needs me, I am there. If He needs me in Sabbath school, to teach children, work with the youth, help adults or just sit and learn. He can use me, because I am there!

I am a soldier. I am not a baby. I do not need to be pampered, petted, primed up, pumped up, picked up or pepped up. I am a soldier.

No one has to call me, remind me, write me, visit me, entice me or lure me. I am a soldier. I am not a wimp. I am in place, saluting my King, obeying His orders, praising His name and building His kingdom!

No one has to send me flowers, gifts, food, cards, candy or give me handouts. I do not need to be cuddled, cradled, cared for or catered to. I am committed.

I cannot have my feelings hurt bad enough to turn me around. I cannot be discouraged enough to turn me aside. I cannot lose enough to cause me to quit. When Jesus called me into this army, I had nothing. If I end up with nothing, I will still come out even.

I will win. My God will supply all my needs. I am more than a conqueror. I will always triumph. I can do all things through Christ.

Devils cannot defeat me. People cannot disillusion me. Weather cannot weary me. Sickness cannot stop me. Battles cannot beat me. Money cannot buy me. Governments cannot silence me and hell cannot handle me!

I am a soldier. Even death cannot destroy me. For when my commander calls me from this battlefield, He will promote me to a captain and then bring me back to rule this world with Him. I am a soldier, in the army, and I'm marching, claiming victory. I will not give up. I will not turn around. I am a soldier, marching heaven bound. Here I stand!

The best for last

Jesus always saves His best for last. Remember the wedding at Cana? When the celebration was about to be ruined because the wine ran out, Jesus called for six jars of water. Now water has very little in common with wine. They're both liquids, but that's about it! Water is colorless, tasteless, and odorless, while wine is red, sweet, and aromatic. But you can see the twinkle in Jesus' eye can't you? He loves making something from nothing. He delights in taking what appears to be useless and turning it into something useful.

The servants pour what moments ago was ordinary well water into the banquet master's cup, and behold! Wine! "Then he called the bridegroom aside and said, 'Everyone brings out the choice wine first and then the cheaper wine after the guests have had too much to drink; but you have saved the best till now' " (John 2:9, 10).

Even as Jesus turned tasteless water into the best wine of the banquet, He is going to transform this impossibly shallow, impossibly self-centered, impossibly distracted, weak, 9:30-living-in-a-midnight-world generation into a people who represent His character more splendidly than any prior generation.

You and I–not the Whites, the Edwards, Muellers, or Moodys—have been chosen to take center stage in the final act of the drama of the ages. And we know that what Jesus saves for last will be His best!

◆ ◆ ◆

A prayer

Lord, teach me to believe that with You all things are possible.
How many times I feel as lifeless as those bones You showed Ezekiel!

Speak to me, Lord. Call me from spiritual death to spiritual life.
Help me not to settle for what is close, "safe," and reachable in my own strength.
What is possible requires no faith.
But help me attempt the impossible–to extend my reach beyond my grasp.
Grant me the capacity to speak words of life to others,
and may I always remember that the greatest miracle of all was
performed 2,000 years ago on a hill called Calvary.
Thank You for Your impossible, unspeakable gift.

---

1. Ellen White, *Christ's Object Lessons*, p. 69.
2. Colin Whittaker, *Great Revivals* (London: William Collins Sons & Co. Ltd, 1990 [1984]), 49.
3. Ellen White, *Steps to Christ*, p.118, 119.
4. *Christ's Object Lessons*, p. 228.
5. Andrew Murray, *Revival* (Minneapolis: Bethany House Publishers, 1990), 28.
6. Jim Cymbala, *Fresh Wind, Fresh Fire* (Grand Rapids: Zondervan Publishing House, 1997), 59.
7. Douglas Cooper, *Living In Our Finest Hour* (Nampa Idaho: Pacific Press Publishing Association, 1982), 14.
8. E. M. Bounds, *The Complete Works of E.M. Bounds on Prayer* (Grand Rapids: Baker Book House, 1990), 376.

It is easy to die for Christ. It is hard to live for him.
Dying takes only an hour or two, but to live for Christ means to die daily.
Only during the few years of this life
are we given the privilege of serving each other and Christ . . .
We shall have heaven forever, but only a short time for service here,
and therefore we must not waste the opportunity.
–Sadhu Sundar Singh

I submit to you that if a man hasn't discovered something
that he will die for, he isn't fit to live."
–Martin Luther King, Jr.

" 'Lazarus, come forth!' "
–John 11:43, NKJV

Revival Generation

Prayers start revivals. So do bullets. In the wake of the Columbine massacre in Littleton, Colorado, a revival of sorts seems to be taking place among our young people. Though the last words of Cassie Bernall are in dispute today, the story of her defiant "Yes" when asked, at gunpoint, if she believed in God, has propelled her to martyr status and stirred a nation.

A *Washington Post* article dated October 14, 1999, captured the feelings of many Christian teens:

> *From the minute the story was reported, it clicked. "The day of the shooting, something popped into my head right then that told me we are the revival generation, that we will go to any extent to say yes to God, even to giving our lives," says Josh Weidmann, a high school senior and founder of Revival Generation, based in Littleton.*
>
> *As time has passed, many Christians have come to think of the Cassie story as proof of God's existence. A cover article in the current issue of Christianity Today argues that Cassie's "heroic yes, with the*

> *muzzle of a gun pressed up against" her, is this generation's defining moment, much as the assassination of President Kennedy and Martin Luther King, Jr. was to the generation before."* [1]

Interestingly enough, signs of revival among teenagers were already gaining national notice long before the Columbine tragedy. The September/October 1998 issue of *Pray!* Magazine focused on teen revival, featuring a cover story entitled "Is This the Generation?: Praying Teens Capture the World for Christ." Events such as "See You at the Pole," and "Challenge 2000"—a plan to plant a student-led prayer/Bible study group on every one of the 56,000 middle, junior high, and high schools in the United States by the end of the year 2000—are indications that something is happening among our youth.

> *Christian teens are praying for their lost friends with a passion. They are getting caught up in the prayer triplet movement—three teens get together and pray for three friends each. They are praying "locker to locker"—for those whose lockers touch theirs. In some areas, students and adults have pioneered "yearbook praying," in which they pray over the names and faces of students in the annual yearbook. Prayerwalking around schools is another aggressive strategy used by youth and youth workers.* [2]

In my own denomination, youth prayer conferences are far outdistancing adult prayer conferences in number and intensity. The work of anointed leaders and friends like Ruthie Jacobsen, Jose Rojas, and Joe Engelkemier is bearing fruit in the lives of young people in every quarter of our division.

A few years ago I attended a prayer conference in Oklahoma and got a front-row seat to the emergence of the Revival Generation. While certain elements of these conferences are always the same (eager, expectant attendees hungry for an encounter with God, intense seasons of prayer, small-group sharing, good music and powerful preaching), Oklahoma featured something different: a separate prayer conference for the youth. While the adults met, worshipped, and prayed in the main building, the young people were doing the same thing across campus, about an eighth of a mile away in the cafeteria complex.

The first reports of what was happening "over there" came from Oklahoma Conference president Rodney Grove and NAD Prayer Conference coordinator Ruthie Jacobsen. We were preparing to conclude the Friday evening worship service when these two "spies" came to the front and told us where they had been the last hour.

"We only intended to poke our heads in the door and give a quick greeting," Ruthie began breathlessly. "They were getting ready to have a season of prayer. They invited us to stay and join the prayer circle. We agreed, thinking we'd only be a few minutes. That was over an hour ago!" Ruthie beamed.

She then went on to describe the most beautiful time of praise and song and confession of sin. Both Rodney and Ruthie shared amazement at the maturity, intensity, and genuineness of the prayers offered by these t-shirt and sandal-clad teenagers.

"But if you could have heard the prayers they prayed for *you!*" Ruthie said. "You would have wept for joy. Tears streamed down my face as I heard them entreat God to bless their parents and send the Spirit to the adults. It was an experience I'll never forget."

The next day during Sabbath School, I watched from the balcony as some forty-plus teens filled the stage and, between songs they performed, shared their testimony. The testimonies were powerful and the entire audience was mesmerized as these kids shared their zeal and enthusiasm for Christ. And these kids weren't just sitting in a circle singing "Kum Ba Yah" all weekend. Their leaders took them into the city in the evenings to the local rescue mission where they ministered nightly to the street people of Oklahoma. Because I was "stuck" with the adults, I didn't get to witness the miracles I later heard took place on these outings, but their faces told the story.

Before our final worship service on Saturday night, Rodney Grove, the speaker for the evening, myself, and other members of the prayer conference team gathered for prayer. As is our custom we encircled the speaker and laid our hands on him. Only this time, we were joined by four young people and one of their leaders. I noted with amusement one young lady vigorously working over a piece of gum just before we prayed. *They're still kids*, I thought and smiled to myself. But when it was her turn to pray, she was all business, and she spoke to God with a confidence and familiarity that most adult Christians would envy. It was a powerful scene—one I won't soon forget. The conference president was encircled by Spirit-filled teenagers who, through the laying on of hands, were petitioning God to fill His servant with power and words from on High.

The next day at the airport, I spotted Peter Neri, one of the adult leaders who worked with the youth. We embraced and before we said our own goodbye, Peter told me about what happened at the youth meeting the night before.

"After your [the adult] meeting was finished, the kids kept going. My ride was waiting for me and I felt so bad holding him up, but they didn't want to stop. If you can imagine a group of teenagers on a Saturday night with their Bibles open, praying, singing, and reading the Word—it was awesome."

Our turn?

Our kids are beginning to say "Yes" to God. Are we? And if we are, what does our Yes mean? What are we saying Yes to? What is the question?

For me, the question I hear my Lord asking is "Do you want to get well?" "Do you want a return of my glory in your life?" "Do you want revival?" And even though I'm not staring down the barrel of a gun as I contemplate my choice, I realize that a Yes answer, like Cassie Bernall's and Rachel Scott's, and so many others before them, will result in death—a death to self.

And it is here I hesitate—and tremble. Why? Because self cries out for mercy! Because self wants to live! Listen, how many of you, after the Columbine shootings had discussions at home or at church about your ability to do what Cassie Bernall did? I wondered, as I'm sure millions of other Christians did, could I have stood up for God with the cold steel of a revolver pressing into my temples? I don't know. I'm certain Cassie didn't know before that final terrifying moment. I believe God gives martyr's faith when martyr's faith is required, not before.

But here's the real deal. Perhaps I'm not sure about my ability to stand for God when faced with a gun because of my poor record of standing for Him when faced with a questionable TV program! Maybe I hesitate saying Yes to God now because of how often I say No to Him on a daily basis. Do you understand what I'm saying? As Christians, we face life and death choices every day—situations that call for us to either crucify self or crucify the Savior afresh. It's Barabbas and Jesus all over again. And how many times, to my shame, have I chosen *Barabbas!*

Perhaps I'm not sure about my ability to stand for God when faced with a gun because of my poor record of standing for him when faced with a questionable TV program!

Revival is not what most of us think it is. Ideas about what true revival is are plenteous. In places like Toronto and Brownsville, Florida, sardonic laughter, uncontrolled sobbing, shaking, roaring like lions, people pinned to the floor stuck in "Holy Ghost glue," and various signs, wonders, and prophetic sayings are touted as the evidences of revival. The emphasis that seems to be winning the day is an esoteric experience—the more bizarre the better.

But "In true revival, neither vivid emotions nor even miraculous healings take precedence over the conviction that the Holy Spirit must give us more inner power to become, like Christ, humble sons and servants, given to the Father's use and disposal, or it is not the truest, purest work of the Spirit at all."[3]

While others look for miracles and manifestations, God is looking for humility and simple faith. While we may want a revival of rapture, the revival we need, and the one God longs to send, is a revival of ***OBEDIENCE***. A revival of spiritual sensitivity and a renewed appetite for the things of God. A revived craving for God's presence and His Word *more* than we crave His blessings. A revival of compassion for the lost. A revival of energy, vision, and courage to ***do*** something—to act on what we hear God saying; to live out in our daily lives what we say we believe.

Virtual revival

But all this is out of step with the times. Our culture is intoxicated with entertainment. More and more theaters with more and more screens, restaurants and shops are being built. Video games get more realistic with graphics that dazzle and stretch the imagination. We live "virtual" lives now, where we're fast losing the ability to discern between what is real and what isn't.

A few years ago while cruising at 30,000 feet on United Airlines, I came across an interesting article about virtual reality in an in-flight magazine. Professor Derrick de Kerchkhove, who teaches French at the University of Toronto and directs the McLuhan Program in Culture and Technology, was discussing the impact of this technology on society. When asked why a tourist would travel to Toronto, presumably to see the city, and then pay to immerse himself in concocted worlds of virtual reality, he responded, "I think that for the moment, reality must be in short supply."

Can this be said of the church today? Is the culture's insatiable appetite for entertainment being manifested in our churches? Are we settling for a "virtual" Christianity because, for the moment at least, the real thing is in short supply? Oh, my friends, let's beware of this mistake!

Remember the seven sons of Sceva? They were going around town trying to "invoke the name of the Lord Jesus over those who were demon-possessed. They would say, 'In the name of Jesus, whom Paul preaches, I command you to come out' " (Acts. 19:13). Notice they said "whom Paul preaches." They didn't know Jesus for themselves. They weren't filled with the Holy Spirit, but they wanted to look like it! So they mimicked what they saw Paul doing and went for the "virtual" experience instead of seeking the real thing. They mouthed words that sounded like the "right" words, and used the techniques that looked like the "right" techniques. And you know what happened. One day, "The evil spirit answered them, 'Jesus I know, and Paul I know about, but who are you?' Then the man who had the evil spirit jumped on them and overpowered them all. He gave them such a beating that they ran out of the house naked and bleeding" (Acts. 19:15, 16).

You might be able to get away with fabricating the New York skyline, or the canals of Venice, or the pyramids of Egypt in the desert of Las Vegas, but you cannot fabricate the glory of Almighty God! A.W. Tozer denounces this type of "virtual" Christianity when he says,

> *The tragic results of this spirit are all about us: Shallow lives, hollow religious philosophies, the preponderance of the element of fun in gospel meetings, the glorification of men, trust in religious externalities, quasi-religious fellowships, salesmanship methods, the mistaking of dynamic personality for the power of the Spirit. . . . For this great sickness that is upon us no one person is responsible, and no Christian is wholly free from blame. We have all contributed, directly*

> *or indirectly, to this sad state of affairs. We have been too blind to see, or too timid to speak out, or too self-satisfied to desire anything better than the poor, average diet with which others appear satisfied. . . . and, worst of all, we have made the Word of Truth conform to our experience and accepted this low plane as the very pasture of the blessed.*[4]

As Israel learned when the ark was captured by the Philistines, the form without the substance is worthless. Where there is no glory of God, the people perish.

The real thing

So what does revival look like? What would be the single greatest manifestation or evidence of the Holy Spirit in our midst? What phenomenon or supernatural happening would be the greatest proof that we were experiencing a Pentecostal outpouring and filling of the Holy Spirit?

I submit that the greatest evidence of a genuine revival will be the presence of agape love. Love for God and love for each other. Why? Because "the fruit of the Spirit is love" (Galatians 5:22). And what I've seen on the faces of the young people and heard coming out of their mouths is a rekindled love for God and for others. The love of God has gotten hold of them and they are constrained to share it with others.

" '*And afterward, I will pour out my Spirit on all people. Your sons and daughters will prophesy, your old men will dream dreams, your young men will see visions. Even on my servants, both men and women, I will pour out my Spirit in those days*' " (Joel 2:28, 29).

The greatest evidence of a genuine revival will be the presence of agape love.

Could we be seeing the fulfillment of Joel's prophecy today? Are the first few drops of the long-awaited Latter Rain outpouring beginning to fall? Commenting on this amazing time, Ellen White writes: "Many . . . will be seen hurrying hither and thither, constrained by the Spirit of God to bring the light to others. The truth, the Word of God, is as a fire in their bones, filling them with a burning desire to enlighten those who sit in darkness . . . . *Children are impelled by the Spirit to go forth and declare the message from heaven.*"[5]

And again: "Before the final visitation of God's judgments upon the earth there will be among the people of the Lord such a revival of primitive godliness as has not been witnessed since apostolic times. The Spirit and power of God will be poured out upon His children."[6]

Was Oklahoma a fluke? Are the prayer conferences that are growing in number and drawing increased interest from around the division a passing fancy? A flash-in-the-pan? Is God really preparing His people to receive the Latter Rain? Only time will tell. But one thing I do know for sure, the promise is being sought after, prayed for, and believed for in these meetings in an unprecedented manner—by old and *young* alike!

"The descent of the Holy Spirit upon the church is looked forward to as in the future; but it is the privilege of the church to have it *now*. Seek for it, pray for it, believe for it. We must have it, and Heaven is waiting to bestow it."[7]

When God's people pray—for revival

When will it happen? Only God knows exactly when the final outpouring will be, but

> *We must not wait for the latter rain. It is coming upon all who will recognize and appropriate the dew and showers of grace that fall upon us. When we gather up the fragments of light, when we appreciate*

> *the sure mercies of God, who loves to have us trust Him, then every promise will be fulfilled [Isaiah 61:11 quoted.] The whole earth is to be filled with the glory of God.* [8]
>
> *There are some who, instead of wisely improving present opportunities, are idly waiting for some special season of spiritual refreshing by which their ability to enlighten others will be greatly increased. They neglect present duties and privileges, and allow their light to burn dim, while they look forward to a time when, without any effort on their part, they will be made the recipients of special blessing, by which they will be transformed and fitted for service.* [9]

In other words, do the small things. Get in the habit of saying "Yes" to God in the small, day-to-day battles of life, and you'll be ready to say "Yes" to Him in the bigger battles to come. Every little "shower" of blessing that comes your way, every drop of heavenly "dew" that falls, gather it up. Don't miss one opportunity to say "Yes" to Jesus—to have His glory manifested through you to someone else. This is what it means to receive the "early rain," and now is the time to get wet.

Now is the time to ask God for the courage to possess the promise of revival. *Now* is the time to beg Him to cure our dry eyes with the healing salve of Heaven's tears. *Now* is the time to obey the insatiable thirst for righteousness that God has created within us. *Now* is the time for churches and individual Christians to do "closet detail" and watch and pray together for a Pentecostal outpouring. *Now* is the time to pray for a heart of compassion that yearns for the salvation of souls, and throbs with love for our brothers and sisters—even those with whom we disagree, and are disagreeable. *Now* is the time to choose Christ over culture, to believe that the Third Angel's Message has the power in it to overcome race prejudice and make us one. *Now* is the time to believe that dry bones can live and that with God, all things are possible. *Now* is the time to ask God for the courage to possess the promise of revival. *Now* is the time to love God more than we love ourselves. *Now is the time for revival!*

Now is the time to ask God for the courage to possess the promise of revial.

Revival Generation

There are no short cuts to revival. Cassie Bernall's "Yes" resulted in her death. But the bullets of April 20, 1999 didn't take her life. Cassie had died long before April 20, when, after having dabbled briefly into the dark world of the occult, she said Yes to Jesus Christ being the Lord of her life. *That* death—the death to self—came first. And because of it, she received the gift of everlasting life that no bullet could take away.

Most of us will not be required to die a martyr's death. For the moment we have the harder task of *living* for Christ, which means dying *daily* to self-righteousness, self-promotion, self-sufficiency, self-centeredness, and self-love. If we truly want to belong to the Revival Generation, that final group of people on earth who "Obey God's commandments and remain faithful to Jesus" (Revelation 14:12), our answer to God will be "Yes," and that "Yes" will shake the heavens and lighten the whole earth with His glory! (Revelation 18:1)

Wake up!

Remember when Jesus told His disciples that He was going to Bethany to wake His friend Lazarus? The disciples, slow to understand as usual, thought that Jesus meant Lazarus was literally asleep and resting—which would be good for his illness. Then Jesus told them plainly: " 'Lazarus is dead' " (John 11:14).

The news must have come as a blow to the disciples. The Lord's friend was dead—beyond hope. But the good news was that Jesus was going to "wake him up."

My friends, Jesus is coming to wake His friends. I'm talking about

His second coming in the clouds when He will say to them that sleep in the dust "Awake." I'm not talking about the literal resurrection. I'm talking about the *spiritual* resurrection of the Church just prior to the physical resurrection that will occur when "the Lord himself will come down from heaven, with a loud command, with the voice of the archangel and with the trumpet call of God, and the dead in Christ will rise first" (1 Thessalonians 4:16.).

Jesus is coming first through the outpouring of the Holy Spirit to rouse His sleeping saints to action so that they can prepare the way of the Lord! If you are one of His sleeping ones, "Awake"! Thy Father calleth thee! Can you not hear His call? We must hear His voice calling us to revival or we'll never hear His voice calling us on resurrection day!

The devil-induced sleep of complacency and busyness has its death grip on us. It is like the bewitching drowsiness described in John Bunyan's classic, *The Pilgrim's Progress*, that nearly overcame Christian and Hopeful when they came to the Enchanted Ground not far from the Celestial City. The two weary pilgrims were so close to their goal—on the very borders of the promised land! But in that pleasant place where the air was always soft and warm, the danger of falling asleep and subsequently being robbed or kidnapped was great.

We too are almost home. All indicators reveal that the great controversy is nearing its end, and like Christian and Hopeful, *we are getting so sleepy!* But Jesus is coming to "wake us." Perhaps you've heard His voice through the pages of this book. I pray that is the case, for it is my only reason for writing it. He's calling your name. Go to Him right now and take possession of the promise.

I will end this book with a prayer that I quoted before in *If My People Pray*. It expresses the heart of every revival-seeking child of God who cries out: "Pass me not O gentle Savior, hear my humble cry. While on others thou art calling, *do not pass me by!*" If this is your cry, then join me in this prayer:

O God, I have tasted Thy goodness, and it has both satisfied me and made me thirsty for more. I am painfully conscious of my need of further grace. I am ashamed of my lack of desire. O God, the Triune God, I want to want Thee; I long to be filled with longing; I thirst to be made more thirsty still. Show me Thy glory, I pray Thee, so that I may know Thee indeed. Begin in mercy a new work of love within me. Say to my soul, 'Rise up, my love, my fair one, and come away.' Then give me grace to rise and follow Thee up from this misty lowland where I have wandered so long. In Jesus' name. Amen.[10]

Lord, *Bring back the glory!*

---

1. Hanna Rosin, "Columbine Miracle: A Matter of Belief; The Last Words of Littleton Victim Cassie Bernall Test A Survivor's Faith–and Charity," *The Washington Post*, Thursday, October 14, 1999, p. C01. Accessed on the Internet: www.washingtonpost.com.
2. I do not know the source of this quote. I wrote it in the flyleaf of my Bible, but failed to note the reference.
3. Doug Tegner, "Revival Streams in a Cultural Desert," *Pray!* Magazine, issue eight, 1998, p. 15.
4. A.W. Tozer, *The Pursuit of God* (Camp Hill, Penn.: Christian Publications, Inc., 1982), 69, 70.
5. Ellen G. White, *Evangelism*, p. 700, emphasis added.
6. Ellen G. White, *The Great Controversy*, p. 464.
7. Ellen G. White, *Review and Herald*, March 19, 1895.
8. *The Seventh-day Adventist Bible Commentary*, vol. 7, p. 984.
9. Ellen G. White, *Acts of the Apostles*, p. 54.
10. A.W. Tozer, *The Pursuit of God* (Camp Hill, Penn.: Christian Publications, Inc., 1982), 20; As quoted in *If My People Pray*, Randy Maxwell (Nampa, Idaho: Pacific Press Publishing Association, 1995), 36.

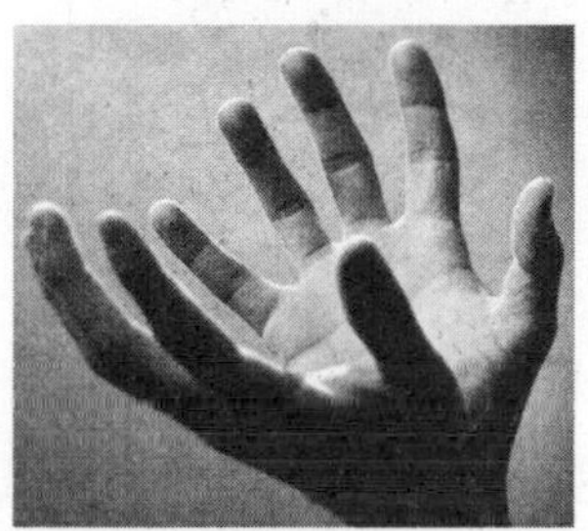

A Final Thought

I'm tired. The last place I want to be right now is in this chair staring at the computer screen and typing these words. I'm exhausted mentally, physically, and spiritually, and to tell the truth, all I really want to do is sack out on my king-sized waterbed which is beckoning me from the open bedroom door across the hall. And though I'm writing about revival, all I want at this moment is to take a nap.

Can you relate? Of course you can. This is life in the "Real World." You feel like this most of the time don't you? I'm guessing the answer is Yes because that's the way it is around here. And I don't think our house is all that different from most households in this new millennium.

I didn't want to end this book without saying something to those of you, who, like myself, want revival, but are having a hard time just getting a good night's sleep. I want you to know that I'm a realist. I don't have my head in the clouds. I wrestle with the same things you do.

If you've never attended one, a prayer conference weekend is a wonderful experience. It's a time of worship, praise, prayer and seeking

6—B.B.G.

God's face for revival. The music is good, the fellowship warm, and the prayer times are intense and uplifting. When coming to the end of such a weekend, I warn my audiences that prayer conferences aren't reality. I'll say something like, "Right now you're pumped, challenged, and highly motivated to change your prayer life. But remember, Monday morning is coming. Tuesday afternoon, and Thursday evening is waiting for you. And when you get there, you won't have your friends or this music, to help you follow through on your resolve."

This book, if it has stirred your heart, is not reality either. The resolve you may be feeling now will be challenged by "real life" real soon.

Life is fast, hopelessly busy. We live our lives in fragments. Major events come and go with the speed of a mouse click on the computer. Graduations, basketball practice, braces, business trips, doctor visits, car trouble, grocery shopping, overdue library books, Sabbath School, shuttling kids back and forth to school, lunches to fix, shots for the dog, book deadlines, jury duty, piano lessons, unexpected house guests, unexpected illnesses, job changes, etc., etc. The demands on our time are incessant and solitude is a fantasy.

When I was co-editor of *ParentTalk* magazine I received the following e-mail message from a writer who was working on an article for me. It reflects what life is like for many of us today.

> *Life has been exceedingly crazy. Tonight is the first time I have had time to get on line since I last communicated with you. There have been two deaths, graduations, major changes at work, weddings, my own brief illness (my body was trying to tell me something), meetings almost around the clock for various groups, two workshops given that were scheduled many months ago. Then I wrote an article that had almost a thousand words too many. I asked my son-in-law to prune it, he did and I will fax the finished piece this week-end and send the hard copy as well. How soon do you need the picture? (I'm ashamed to*

let you see who I am. :-)) I have simply not had the time to have one taken. I leave for Maryland this coming Wednesday evening, after seeing my clients. I will be driving with my nephew who is headed for Graduate School at Howard and needs to get his car and personal belongings there as well. I return to SF on July 8. If you need the picture before then I will do everything possible to comply, even if that means having the picture taken during the week I am in Maryland.

In any event if you are still speaking to me, my home phone number is . . . , work number . . . , pager . . . , fax . . . , work fax . . . . You may call any time. I generally leave for work between 6-6:30 a.m. and return home, depending on the day of the week and what meeting I have scheduled after work, somewhere between 9:00 p.m. - 12:01 a.m.

I know, I am a workaholic and intemperate but I decided a long time ago that I prefer to wear out rather than rust out.

Don't you just love that last line? "I prefer to wear out rather than rust out." Either way, you're out! And you know what? "Out" is exactly where Satan wants us to be. The following fictional story has been circulating via e-mail for a long time now, and to my knowledge, the author is unknown. However, the point is well taken.

Satan called a worldwide convention. In his opening address to his evil angels, he said, "We can't keep the Christians from going to church. We can't keep them from reading their Bibles and knowing the truth. We can't even keep them from conservative values. But we can do something else.

"We can keep them from forming an intimate, abiding experience in Christ. If they gain that connection with Jesus, our power over them is broken. So let them go to church. Let them have their conservative lifestyles, but steal their time so they can't gain that

experience in Jesus Christ. This is what I want you to do, angels. Distract them from gaining hold of their Savior and maintaining that vital connection throughout their day!"

"How shall we do this?", shouted his angels.

"Keep them busy in the non-essentials of life and invent unnumbered schemes to occupy their minds," he answered. "Tempt them to spend, spend, spend, then borrow, borrow, borrow. Convince the wives to go to work, and the husbands to work six or seven days a week, 10-12 hours a day, so they can afford their lifestyles. Keep them from spending time with their children. As their family fragments, soon, their homes will offer no escape from the pressures of work.

"Over stimulate their minds so that they cannot hear that still, small voice. Entice them to play the radio or cassette player whenever they drive, to keep the TV, the VCR, and their CDs going constantly in their homes. And see to it that every store and restaurant in the world plays music constantly. This will jam their minds and break that union with Christ.

"Fill their coffee tables with magazines and newspapers. Pound their minds with the news 24 hours a day. Invade their driving moments with billboards. Flood their mailboxes with junk mail, sweepstakes, mail order catalogs, and every kind of newsletter and promotional offering free products, services and false hopes.

"Even in their recreation, let them be excessive. Have them return from their recreation exhausted, disquieted and unprepared for the coming week. Don't let them go out in nature. Send them to amusement parks, sporting events, concerts and movies instead. And when they meet for spiritual fellowship, involve them in gossip and small talk so that they leave with troubled consciences and unsettled emotion.

"Let them be involved in soul winning, but crowd their lives with so many good causes they have no time to seek power from Christ. Soon they will be working in their own strength, sacrificing their

health and family unity for the good of the cause."

It was quite a convention in the end. And the evil angels went eagerly to their assignments causing Christians everywhere to get busy, busy, busy and rush here and there.

The story is fiction, but the facts behind it are too true. Writing in the book *Education*, Ellen White observed,

An intensity such as never before was seen is taking possession of the world. In amusement, in money-making, in the contest for power, in the very struggle for existence, there is a terrible force that engrosses body and mind and soul. In the midst of this maddening rush, God is speaking.[1]

Busyness and fatigue may be among the greatest challenges the "Revival Generation" will face in these closing hours of earth's history. God is speaking, but can we hear Him? **How can I experience revival when all I want to do is take a nap?**

Let me suggest three things that might help us all.

1. Get some sleep.

Recent national surveys reveal that millions of Americans are terribly sleep deprived. (You didn't need a survey to tell you that, did you?) Forty percent of adults say that they are so sleepy during the day that it interferes with their daily activities. [2] (You're probably one of them!)

Maybe you're like my wife. She's on the go from the time her feet hit the floor in the morning until her head hits the pillow at night (usually around midnight!). She spins and spins never allowing herself time to stop. But the moment she sits or lays down, she's fast asleep. When you're that tired, it's nearly impossible to have a productive "quiet time" in prayer and in God's Word. Thirty seconds into your Bible reading, and the words start runningtogetherinablobandbeforeyouknowityou'refastasleeeeeee....

Follow Elijah's example and get some sleep. After a big day on Mt. Carmel—praying fire and rain down from heaven, killing the prophets of Baal, and running faster than Ahab's chariot all the way to Jezreel—Elijah got word that Jezebel had taken out a contract on his life. He then ran "a day's journey into the desert" to escape the Queen. There, exhausted and depressed, this mighty man of God prayed for death and then "fell asleep" (1Kings 19:4, 5).

Read the story carefully and you'll see that God didn't chastise Elijah for his depression or his suicidal prayer. He knew that what Elijah needed was rest and refreshment. So do we. Start paying attention to your sleep habits. Stick to a regular schedule for going to bed and waking up, even on weekends. Give yourself permission to lie down and get some rest. That's right, go ahead, take your nap. Schedule it. Set you alarm and go for that much needed sleep. Only promise yourself that as part of that nap, you will awaken, not to the next item on your "To Do" list, but to a period of silence and solitude with the Lord. If you're refreshed and alert, your mind and spirit will be receptive to the voice of God.

2. Learn to say "No."

This is a tough one for me, but since turning 40 last year, my wife says I can say No more often. (She even told me to practice saying it in front of the mirror!) I'm not advocating the wholesale abandonment of all your church duties, etc., but I am urging that you use greater discretion. How many things are you currently doing only out of fear of disappointing others, or fear of not being needed? How many of your current activities do you secretly resent? Pray for and exercise discernment—that spiritual ability to choose what is best over what is merely good. Saying No is an effective means of de-cluttering your life. You'll have more time to slow down, to be alone, pour out your overburdened heart to God and admit your desperate need for inner refreshment.

3. Be Quiet

I can't say this strongly enough. *Silence is indispensable if we hope to add depth to our spiritual life.* In his book, *Intimacy with the Almighty,* Charles Swindoll writes, "Noise and words and frenzied, hectic schedules dull our senses, closing our ears to His still, small voice and making us numb to His touch."[3]

Last summer our family spent a few hours in Utah's Zion National Park. We gasped and oohed and aahed at the magnificent red rock formations that towered above us. But it was the silence combined with the visual spectacle that made us feel God's awesome presence. Three hours down I-15 we were in Las Vegas. Talk about a contrast! Amid the orgy of noise, pleasure seeking, and sensory stimulation of that place, it was easy to see how the still, small voice of God would be difficult to hear.

You can't control the noise of the world around you, but you can turn down the volume of your own inner space. Make room for quiet in your life. Unplug the phone. Shut off the TV. Turn off the radio or CD player and spend some time every day in silence. I won't kid you. This will be very difficult to do. There were times during the writing of this book when, despite being alone in my living room, the washing machine in the laundry room next door would be chugging away, and the sounds of my kid's *Adventures in Odyssey* tapes would float down the hall.

It's hard to filter out the noise. But we must try, for intimacy is best developed in silence where distractions are reduced and we can focus giving our full attention to God.

I know that no amount of clever illustrations showing how busy we are will make us change. I am often humbled and convicted by such illustrations like the one about Satan's convention. But after smiling and acknowledging that they hit close to home, I file them away and keep right on my "gerbil-like" pace of life. So, I'm not asking you to change your habit patterns—only God can pull that off. (He's Lord of the impossible, remember?) But if we will take some basic "baby" steps and come to God with our busy schedules, He'll show us how to escape the pit of exhaustion that threatens our walk with Him.

The person who looks out at you from your mirror is the one in need of prayer and revival. Get some rest and then start the journey . . . on your knees.

---

1. Ellen White, *Education*, p. 260.
2. "How Sleepy Are You? 1999 U.S. Sleep Survey Shows Disturbing Trends in Daytime Sleepiness," www.sleepfoundation.org/PressArchives/lead.html
3. Charles Swindoll, *Intimacy with the Almighty*(Dallas, Tex.: Word Publishing, Inc., 1996), 38, 39.

Bring Back the GLORY

Introduction:

9:30 Living in a Midnight World

1. If Christ's second coming is represented by "midnight," then as far as your own readiness to meet Him, where do you place yourself on the clock?

2. If you're in a group, discuss your answer and explain why you chose the time you did.

3. What words and/or mental images come to your mind when you think of "revival"? Write them down.

4. Compare your responses with James Burns's statement: "A revival has ever been unpopular with large numbers within the church. Because it says nothing to them of power such as they have learned to love, or of ease, or of success; it accuses them of sin, it tells them that they are dead, it calls them to awake, to renounce the world, and to follow Christ."

5. What are the similarities or differences between your picture of revival and Burns's picture? Write or discuss these.

6. Take a few moments to write down or discuss your reaction to the Ellen White statement in *Christ's Object Lessons*: "Christ is waiting with longing desire for the manifestation of Himself in His Church. When the character of Christ shall be perfectly reproduced in His people, then He will come to claim them as His own."

7. Read Asaph's prayer in Psalm 80:7, 18, and add your own feelings to it. Write your prayer in a journal. If you're in a group, pray through verses 1-3, 7, 14, 18, 19.

Study Questions

Chapter 1:
The Undiscovered Country

1. Put yourself in the spies' place as they surveyed the land of Canaan. Do you identify more with Caleb and Joshua, or with the ten who doubted? Why?

2. The author says that we've been afraid of the Holy Spirit too long. That we've associated the *experience* of the Holy Spirit with the *excesses* of emotionalism to the point that we settle for theoretical knowledge. Do you agree or disagree? Explain.
Take time to answer the series of questions the author poses on pages 23 and 24. Pray about them first, then write or discuss your answers in your group.

Chapter 2:
Where's the Glory?

1. What does the statement, "Let us fetch the ark of the covenant of the Lord out of Shiloh unto us . . ." (1 Sam. 4:3) reveal about Israel's relationship to the ark at this time?

2. What is the meaning of the word "Ichabod"?

3. Why did Phinehas's wife give her son this name?

4. Look up 1 Samuel 3:1. What's the meaning of the phrase "In those days the word of the Lord was rare (or "precious" in the KJV)?

5. Why weren't the people seeing God?

6. Discuss why, according to a 1991 Gallup poll, there is a glaring lack of Bible knowledge in America.

7. Think about your own pace of life. How much time do you take for Bible reading/study? Is God's Word becoming "rare" in your life? From the examples of Moses, Isaiah, and Saul, what are at least three responses to seeing the Lord?

(1)____

(2)____

(3)____

8. Discuss C. William Fetcher's statement: "It is not enough for any generation to be told about the great revivals of the past. There must be a fresh baptism with fire for the sons and daughters, and the atmosphere of revival must prevail in every new day until the Son of Man shall come." Is this true? In your opinion does our church look back more than it looks forward? Discuss the pros and cons of your answer.

9. "When they looked upon the ____________ and did not associate it with _______, nor ________________________ His revealed will by ____________________ to His law, it could avail them little more than a common ____________. . . . It was not enough that the ________ and the ____________________________ were in the midst of____________________. It was not enough than the __________________ offered sacrifices, and that the people were called the ______________________ or _____________. The Lord __________ ________ regard the request of those who cherish ____________________ in the heart." (PP, 584)

10. Discuss the definitions of revival on page 39. Is revival something you need to experience personally? Why or why not?

11. List and discuss the seven spiritual indicators that revival is needed.

(1)____

(2)____

(3)____

(4)____

(5)____

(6)____

(7)____

12. Read the questions asked by revivalist Charles G. Finney on page 44. How do you feel as you contemplate them? If alone, write your answers in a journal. If in a group, discuss your answers and end in prayer.

Chapter 3:
The Glory of Brokenness

1. Describe spiritual Dry Eye Syndrome.

2. Revival eludes us because

____

____

3. Can you relate to the author's experience of brokenness? (See pages 48 and 49) Have you felt like this recently? What were the circumstances? Do you see this as positive or negative? Explain.

4. Compare Joel 2:28, 29 with Joel 2:12-17 and discuss the means God expects His people to use in pursuing revival.

5. "This is why a ______________ has ever been ________________ with large numbers within the ______________. Because it says nothing to them of ____________, such as they have learned to love, or of ____________, or of ________________; it ________________ them of _______, it tells them that they are _________, it calls them to ________________, to ______________ the world, and to follow

____________________." —James Burns

6. Discuss what the "Sacred Assembly" is and how it would look in your church. What would need to be different for: (A) the pastor (B) the elders and church leaders (C) the musicians (D) members

7. What is it about a broken spirit and a contrite heart (Psa. 51:17) that God likes?

8. Read the letter by Bakht Singh describing American Christianity (page 54). Though written in the 1960s, is this still an accurate description of the church today? How closely does it describe your church?

9. Consider the author's statement: "With churches splitting over power issues, pastors becoming entangled in illegal financial schemes, racial prejudice keeping members at arm's length with each other, and endless struggles over positions and control, it would appear as if the closer Jesus gets to returning, the further His people get from repenting." Do you agree or disagree? Explain.

10. Read Mark 10:43-45, then answer these questions: (1) "Is servanthood on your agenda?" (2) "Are you willing to stay right where you are and let

the Lord do great things through you, though nobody seems to care or notice at all?"

11. Compare the attitudes of Moses, Paul, and Jesus in Exod. 32:31, 32; Rom. 9:2, 3, and Phil. 2:6-8 with your own. How willing are you to surrender your "rights" to help lift up your brother or sister?

12. Discuss the author's idea of "Basin Theology." How could this work in your church? Do you know of relationships in the church that would be benefited by this gesture of humility and acceptance?

13. Read Wilbur Rees's poem on pages 59 and 60. How much of yourself do you see in this poem? Pray about what God reveals to you through this question.

NOTE: Join an online Sacred Assembly by posting your prayer for repentance and revival at http://www.tagnet.org/ifmypeoplepray.

Chapter 4:
The Glory of Prevailing Prayer

1. If prayer is such a mighty weapon, why do we, in the words of Charles Spurgeon, permit it to "rust"?

2. Discuss times when prayer is "a spitting, cussing, sweating, blister-breaking enchilada, with extra cramps."

3. Read the story of the invalid man at the pool of Bethesda (John 5:1-15). Go over this story verse by verse, asking *Who, What, When, Where,* and *Why* questions as you go. Finish with a prayer for insight into what God may be saying to you through this story. Share your insights with the group (or write them in your prayer journal).

4. Share a time when you were either *really* thirsty or *really* hungry. What were the circumstances? How did it feel?

5. What's the good news about spiritual thirst?

6. Why do many prayer meetings fizzle?

7. Could the title: *We Wrestle Not!* be applied to you or your church? Why or why not?

8. Read Luke 11:1-13 and 18:1-8. What do these parables teach us about the role of intensity, desire, and need in prayer?

9. Discuss the role of unity in revival. What's the meaning of the disciples being "all with one accord in one place" (Acts 2:1).

10. Why is it so easy for Christians to break ranks with each other?

11. Do we have any "substance" or "evidence" for revival on which we can hang our prayers? What is it?

12. How is praying for revival like running a marathon?

Bring Back the GLORY

Chapter 5:
The Glory of Waiting

1. Read the prayer that the author copied down in his prayer journal (see pages 79 and 80). Do you identify with it? How so?

2. What are the benefits of fasting? When was the last time you fasted? What were the circumstances and what were the results?

3. What is "The Concert of Prayer"? Could this plan work in your church or district?

4. What is a "closet" Concert of Prayer? Pray and ask God if He's calling you to begin a closet concert of prayer with someone who shares your burden for revival.

5. Discuss the possibilities, benefits, and challenges of a daily prayer meeting in your church.

6. Discuss the author's assertion that "We need to start expecting God to impact us beyond the confines of the church bulletin!" What do you think he means by this? How does this relate to your church?

7. List three reasons why perseverance in prayer is necessary.

Bring Back the GLORY

Chapter 6:
The Glory of Compassion

1. Discuss the author's statement: "With all my heart I believe that one of the reasons God can't bless our evangelism with greater results is because our love for the lost is programmed." What's your reaction to this statement? Is it true in your church's case?

2. Are you "losing sleep" over the spiritual condition of your neighbors?

3."The trouble with many ____________________ is that they get _______________ over ______________ and are __________________ about tragedies. They are _________________ because of some personal slight, but are __________-_________ while the wolves of lust devour our youth and while ______________ of ______________ _____________ scatter the flock." —Leonard Ravenhill
From your own experience, how have you seen this statement reflected in your church?

4. If your church suddenly disappeared, how long do you think it would take the neighbors to notice? Discuss the ramifications of your answer.

5. Please discuss this series of questions: "How can we claim to be "ready"

for Jesus to come, when so many of those around us—including friends and loved ones—aren't ready to meet Him? Why doesn't this bother us more than it does? Do we really believe Jesus is coming? Do we really believe there's a heaven and a second death? Do we believe that without a saving knowledge of Christ, many will perish needlessly? Do we care?"

6. Read Isa. 58:6, 7. What is the "Lord's fast"?

7. What are the consequences of settling for "good church" or "respectable Christianity"?

8. What is "disinterested love"?

9. What is prayer-walking? What would it take for this to be implemented in the neighborhood around your church? Could you see yourself in this ministry?

10. Pray through the prayer at the end of the chapter and journal the feelings you have concerning the lost.

Chapter 7:
The Glory of Reconciliation

1. Does the subject of racism seem out of place in a discussion about revival? Explain.

2. The author says: "If our faith doesn't challenge us on those areas that touch us at the core of our being, it isn't worth much." Do you agree or disagree? Explain.

3. Does a revived church have to be a "racially reconciled church"? Explain.

4. Why did the remnant church stop being a "peculiar people" when it came to the race issue?

5. Have you personally had the experience of explaining our separate conference structure to a new or non-member? What was their reaction? How did you feel as you tried to explain this?

6. What is the supreme theme of your faith? Is it Christ or culture? How do you know?

7. What accounts for the Rwanda holocaust?

8. Discuss the author's assertion that, "For Christ's sake, we must learn to trust and love each other, for this will surely be the greatest evidence of a truly Holy Ghost revival among us. Not baptisms, but brotherhood. Not an increase in tithe, but an increase of trust."

9. Do you have prejudices and hold negative stereotypes against others that keep you from developing meaningful relationships with members of another ethnic group? Are you willing to confess these feelings to God?

10. How many people unlike yourself form your inner circle? What would it take for you to develop a friendship with somebody who is different from you?

11. Discuss the benefits, challenges or difficulties of arranging a pastor swap with a church of a different ethnicity. How about a joint prayer service? How feasible would this be in your situation?

12. Discuss Spencer Perkins's statement: "Christianity doesn't require any power when its only challenge is doing something that already comes

naturally. But it will take a powerful gospel—a gospel with guts—to enable us to love across all the barriers we erect to edify our own kind and protect us from our insecurities."

Study Questions

Chapter 8:

The Glory of the Impossible

1. Discuss G. K. Chesterton's statement: " Christianity has not been tried and found wanting. It has been found difficult and left untried. " What's true and false about this statement?

2. Do you ever wonder how God is going to perfectly reproduce His character in us? Does it seem impossible at times? When does it appear this way to you?

3. Read Ezek. 37:1-14. Go over this story of the Dry Bones verse by verse, asking *Who, What, When, Where,* and *Why* questions as you go. Finish with a prayer for insight into what God may be saying to you through this story. Share your insights with the group (or write them in your prayer journal).

4. Explain Ezekiel's hesitation. Have you been there? Share your experience.

5. The word for "prophesy" in Hebrew is ____________. It means ____________________.

6. Read Eph. 4:29. What would happen in your church if the spirit of criticism were placed by the spirit of encouragement?

7. What two things brought the bones to life?
(1)____

(2)____

8. Compare hearing and doing in the Jewish mind.

9. Read Ezek. 33:30-32. How is the church like this today?

10. What two lessons about revival does this vision of the Dry Bones teach?
(1)____

(2)____

Chapter 9:
Revival Generation

1. How is saying "Yes" to God for revival similar to Cassie Bernall's "Yes" before she was killed?

2. While others look for miracles and manifestations, what is God looking for?

3. How does our culture's intoxication with entertainment manifest itself in the church?

4. What was the mistake of the sons of Sceva (see Acts 19:13-17)? How can we avoid this same mistake?

5. Discuss A.W. Tozer's statement on pages 153 and 154. Do you agree or disagree? Explain.

6. In the opinion of the author, what's the greatest evidence of a genuine revival? Do you agree or disagree? Explain.

7. Are we to wait for the Latter Rain? Why or why not?

8. Are you ready to say "Yes" to God about revival? If not, ask God in prayer to give you the courage to take this step. If yes, ask God to fill you with His Spirit and make you an agent of revival in your home, church, and neighborhood. Read the prayer at the end of the chapter, then express your feelings to God in your own words.

Study Questions

A Final Thought

1. Read the e-mail that the author received when he was co-editor of *ParentTalk* magazine. In what ways does your life resemble this letter?

2. Take time to write out your answer to the question: "How can I experience revival when all I want to do is take a nap?"

If you enjoyed this book, you'll enjoy these as well:

If My People Pray
Randy Maxwell. What would happen in our homes, churches, and communities if we followed God's counsel in 2 Chronicles 7:14, humbled ourselves, and prayed? This book shows how to experience prayer as relationship, power, and the key to revival.
English, 0-8163-1246-X. Paperback. US$10.99, Can$15.99.
Spanish, 1-5755-4031-2. Paperback. US$6.99, Can$9.99.

On Eagles' Wings
Randy Maxwell. Life can tend to weigh you down with worry, fear, and impatience. Jesus wants to help us get above our daily trials and claim victory over our difficulties. *On Eagles' Wings* offers a sensible nuts-and-bolts approach to daily Christian living that will inspire you to take action.
0-8163-1345-8. Paperback. US$4.99, Can$6.99.

. . . And this exciting companion product to ***Bring Back the Glory***:

Standing in the Need of Prayer
The Carnies. Twelve songs of **A**doration, **C**onfession, **T**hanksgiving, and **S**upplication to revive the heart that longs to pray. Listeners are lead on a personal journey to the throne of grace through songs like "In the Presence of Jehovah," "Standing in the Need of Prayer," "Give Thanks (medley)," "My Jesus, I Love Thee," "Holy Ghost Revival," and more. Inspiring narrations from *If My People Pray* author Randy Maxwell included.
CD: 4333002270; CS: 4333002271. CD: US$15.98, Cdn$23.99; CS: $10.98, Cdn$16.49.

Order from your ABC by calling **1-800-765-6955**, or get online and shop our virtual store at **www.adventistbookcenter.com**.

Read a chapter from your favorite book
Order online
Sign up for e-mail notices on new products